**LOOK EVELYN,
DUCK DYNASTY WIPER BLADES.
WE SHOULD GET THEM.**

ISBN 978-0-9886895-2-7
Look Evelyn, Duck Dynasty Wiper Blades. We Should Get Them.
A Collection Of New Essays

david@27bslash6.com

Also available by the same author:

The Internet is a Playground
Published by Penguin, *The Internet is a Playground* is the first release by David Thorne. Making its debut at #4 on The New York Times bestseller list, it includes articles from 27bslash6 plus over 160 pages of new material. It makes a nice present, protects against tigers, and can be read while hiding in small places.

I'll Go Home Then; It's Warm and Has Chairs
Featuring articles from 27bslash6.com along with brand-spanking-new material, *I'll Go Home Then; It's Warm and Has Chairs* is the second book release by author David Thorne and is available now.

For Seb and Holly. All the reasons.

Contents

Foreword

"What's the new book about?" my friend JM asked recently, "Is it going to have lots of new emails?"

"No," I told him, "I thought I'd put together a collection of articles, essays if you will, rather than emails this time."

"Oh, I like the emails," he said disappointed, "there's not going to be any? Not even one?"

"Maybe one."

"Good. I like the emails. Remember that one you did about the spider? Fuck that was funny."

"That was over five years ago," I replied, "I've posted a lot of stuff since then."

"Yes, but they haven't been as good as the spider one. You should do more emails about spiders."

"Yes, perhaps the new book should consist only of emails about spiders. Or I could just repeat the same story every ten pages or so. That would save me a lot of time."

"You could mix it up a bit. Maybe send a real spider. Or a whole box of them."

"By email?"

"No, by normal mail. Their reaction when they open the box would be priceless."

"Yes, but I wouldn't be there to see it."

"Doesn't matter, it would still be funny."

"So the entire book should be about sending people boxes of live spiders and imagining their reaction to opening it?"

"I'd read it."

Cabbages

There is a small island off the southern tip of the Great Andaman archipelago, shaped a bit like a slice of bread, called North Sentinel Island. Nobody knows what the people living on North Sentinel Island call the island because the inhabitants, noted for resisting all attempts at contact by outsiders, are more interested in throwing spears than chatting.

They maintain a society subsisting through hunting, fishing, and collecting wild plants. There is no evidence of either agricultural practices or methods of producing fire and their language remains unknown.

Every twenty years or so, anthropologists attempt to coax the islanders from their hostile reception of outsiders by leaving coconuts on the beach and waving from boats anchored just beyond spear-throwing distance. Sometimes the natives wave back and the anthropologists, encouraged, approach close enough to be speared.

Which is why I call my desk North Sentinel Island II.

I made my own flag, by drawing a pair of crossed spears on a blank timesheet, and flew it from my desk using sticky-tape and a ruler.

"What's the X stand for?" asked Kevin.

Kevin, an account manager at the design agency I work for, makes regular attempts at contact with North Sentinel Island II but instead of offering coconuts, he offers lengthy tales of how well his cabbages are growing and the soil conditions required for such.

"It's not an X," I informed him, "It's two spears crossing over each other."

I've never been overly adept at drawing. It might be assumed that some degree of artistic aptitude is required to work in the design industry but there is a vast difference between pencil on paper and pixels on screen. I can split paths and know the names of far too many typefaces, but I would be the last person I'd pick as a partner on Pictionary night.

"Is it a person rollerskating during a tornado?"
"No, it's a grape."

When I was nine, I drew a picture in class of my dog Gus jumping into a pond. The teacher mistook it for an excellent picture of a snake coming out of a cave and I was somehow elected to participate in the painting of a school mural depicting wildlife preservation. Featured in the school corridor for the next four years, between fairly decent representations of an ostrich and elephant by students with a modicum of talent, was what became known as *David's egg-flip with eyes.*

"It looks more like an X," Kevin critiqued, "If you made the pointy bits more profound, like they were made out of sharpened rocks, and added bits of cloth hanging down where the rocks are tied to the sticks, they would look a lot more like spears."

"Right, thank you for the suggestion, Kevin. I should probably have consulted you on correct spear drawing techniques prior to undertaking the design. What can I help you with?"

"Nothing," he replied, scrolling through his iPhone, "I just wanted to show you something..."

"Is it a photo of a cabbage?" I asked, "I've already seen it."

"No, hang on... wait, that's not it... that's my daughter's eldest at his graduation ceremony, nice kid, top marks in his class... hang on... I know it's here somewhere..."

"I'm fairly busy at the moment..." I tried interjecting.

"Here it is... no, wait, that's not it either..."

I tried growing my own vegetables once, after watching a program called Prepping in which people with beards and Wrangler jeans anticipate social collapse. I paid around $30 for seeds, $100 for railway ties, and $250 for fifty bags of garden soil which means the two cucumbers I ended up with cost $190 each. They weren't even good cucumbers. One was about two inches in length and the other had a huge grub living inside it.

Should the grid ever 'go down', I estimate my chances of long-term survival as slim at best. I'll probably be shot at the supermarket and have my cans of evaporated milk and instant coffee taken from me on the first day.

My coworker Simon once told me that he really wished there would be a zombie apocalypse like in the show, *The Walking Dead*.

"I'd use a bow, or crossbow," he said, "Like Darryl. Because it's quieter."

"Sure," I agreed, "But the reload is dreadful. You'd probably be better off with a shotgun. Even if it is a bit louder. You don't have to be a very good aim with a shotgun."

Simon smiled and shook his head, "That's why I'd be a main character and you'd be one of the new people that joins our community then gets bitten and turns into a zombie that I have to shoot. With an arrow."

When I was ten, I shot my dog Gus with an arrow. It wasn't on purpose though and he didn't die or anything. He just ran around the yard yelping with the arrow in his hind leg for a bit until my mother came out to see what all the noise was about. I'd built the bow out of a branch and packaging twine. Lacking actual feathers to use as stabilisers for the arrows, I attached a leaf to the end of a fairly straight stick with tape, and sharpened the other end. Upon testing, I found it almost impossible to draw back the taught string, so I laid on my back, placed both feet in the bow with the arrow between, and pulled with both hands. With my arms and legs quivering from the strain and the string cutting deep into my fingers, I aimed towards a box sitting on top of a stump. The box had concentric circles drawn on it but instead of giving each a number, I'd written the names of all the people in my class who called me by the nickname 'Egg-flip'. With my bent knees about to give out, I pushed just a bit a harder... and my legs locked straight up, ripping the string from my grip. Due to the high angle of trajectory, the arrow travelled perhaps sixty feet in height but only twenty in distance. Gus was lying on his side in the grass, enjoying the sun, when the arrow hit.

I wasn't punished by my parents for the incident but I did have to listen to the "We're not angry, we're just disappointed" speech on the way to the vet. My parents were never really big on discipline. The only physical punishment I remember receiving was having my mouth washed out with soap. I was seven. My father switched channels to the news while I was watching The Goodies and, having heard a term that day at school and assuming it was a generic one like ragamuffin or boofhead, I called him a cocksucker. Dragged down the hallway and into the bathroom, what I recall of the punishment was not the taste of the soap, but the fact that the only bar available was a mushy blob stuck to the tiled floor of the shower. As I spat the soap, and a toenail, into the sink afterwards, I remember thinking, 'Nobody in our family has short curly hair, whose hair is this?'

During a recent discussion with my father about bad

parenting, I reminded him of this and he replied, "Bullshit. It was Brut-33 soap-on-a-rope. It was hanging on the tap. That's what the rope is for you fucking liar."

Gus walked with a limp for the rest of his life. Which wasn't very long as he was run over by a truck a few weeks later. He probably couldn't hobble out of the way in time. We buried him in the backyard but my father dug him up a few months later when we put in a pool. He still had the bandage on his hind leg and a note under his collar that read, "Dear Gus, Sorry for shooting you in the leg with an arrow. You were a good dog. Except when you stood in front of the TV."

"Ah, here it is!" declared Kevin finally. He held up the screen to show me a photo of a cabbage.
"You showed me that yesterday," I remarked, "and I told you at the time that if I wanted to look at pictures of cabbages I would type 'pictures of cabbages' into Google."
"It's a different photo," he explained, "look how much they've grown in just a few days."
A photo of a cabbage growing in soil, without something in the photo for scale, such as a banana, could be two inches or two feet across. I pointed this out to Kevin.
Kevin looked at the photo and frowned, "You're a fucking idiot," he said on his way out.

After he left, I made the pointy bits on my flag look like sharpened rocks and added bits of cloth where they joined the sticks. It did actually look better but then I tried adding blood to the end of the spears with a red whiteboard marker which made the spears look like match sticks wearing ties so I had to redo the entire thing.

The phone on my desk rang.

"North Sentinel Island II tourist information. This is David. How can I help you?"
"What?" Melissa asked, "Is Kevin up there? Ben's on hold for him."

Melissa replaced our previous secretary - or 'front desk manager' as Sharon had preferred to be called - a few years back after what is commonly referred to as the Recipient Incident.

Mistakenly selecting 'Staff' instead of her boyfriend 'Steve', Sharon sent a selfie of herself wearing only pigtails to everyone in the office. Being fat - or 'curvy' as fat people prefer to be called - the thing that impressed me most about the selfie was her flexibility. There is no way I could get my feet behind my head, even with a pillow under my back like she had. I've tried.

While I can understand Sharon's decision to leave without notice, the subject matter was actually less embarrassing than the environment the photo was taken in. Her bedroom had green striped wallpaper and a ruffled floral bedspread. A stained glass lamp shaped like a butterfly was just visible amongst a throng of teddy bears on her side table and above her bed was a poster of a tiger. Who lives like this? If it was my bedroom, I wouldn't be taking nude selfies, I would be weeping as I splashed kerosene about and lit a match.

I was actually glad when she left. The only bathroom is across the hall from my office and Sharon apparently suffered from Irritable Bowel Syndrome. It wasn't the noise, which was like twenty sauce bottles being simultaneously squeezed to the last drop, but the fact that she would leave the door open after finishing. Almost every time, I would have to get up, walk through her Agent-Orange-like mist, and close the door.

"Can we try keeping this door closed please?" I once asked.
"Sorry," Sharon replied sarcastically.
"Yes, I don't think you are actually sorry otherwise you'd close the door and not subject everyone to what smells like a large pile of dead cats. Dead cats covered in shit. The 'Fresh Linen' Febreeze doesn't mask the odour, it just makes it smell like a large pile of dead cats covered in shit with a dryer-sheet stuck on top."
"You're so rude," she replied, "I can't help it if I have Irritable Bowel Syndrome. It's a medical condition."

From: Jennifer Haines
To: David Thorne
Subject: Complaint

David,

Sharon has filed a F26-A in regards to comments you allegedly made about a medical condition she suffers from. Under section 3, paragraph 8 of the Employee Workplace Agreement it states that no employee will be discriminated against for any medical condition. Please keep your opinions to yourself in future. Irritable Bowel Syndrome is a real condition.

Jennifer

....

From: David Thorne
To: Jennifer Haines
Subject: Re: Complaint

Dear Jennifer,

I'm sure it is but if I were to bother looking up the symptoms, I doubt they would include an inability to close doors. Besides, I'm fairly sure dropping the fecal equivalent of Hiroshima every few hours has more to do with diet than disorders. I once saw her eat a cake for lunch. Not a cupcake or a large slice of cake, a whole cake. If someone of normal weight defecated with the regularity and magnitude of Sharon's seismic dumps, they would be dead within the day. It would be like an average sized dog giving birth to a cow.

Regards, David

....

"No," I answered Melissa, "I think Kevin went out."
'Right." Click.

This was pretty much the extent of Melissa's phone etiquette. She hadn't been employed based on experience. Despite a sign on the front window stating, 'No Soliciting', various people often enter off the street asking if anyone wants to buy things from a big bag. The items are usually cheap electronics, memo holders, flashlight keychains. That sort of thing. I like it when they come in. The day after Sharon left, a girl in her early twenties came in lugging her bag of wares. It was raining outside and she looked miserable.

"Hello, my name is Melissa and I was wondering if anyone in this office would be interested in purchasing items from a fabulous selection of fabulous gifts and gadgets?"
"Do they make you say that?" I asked.
"Yes."
"You said the word fabulous twice. Was it supposed to be 'a fabulous selection' or 'fabulous gifts and gadgets'?"

"Fabulous gifts and gadgets," she answered, "It's my first day."

"How's it working out? Are you selling lots of gifts and gadgets?"

"No."

"Do you want a better job?"

She doesn't have to do much. Apart from answering and redirecting the occasional incoming call, she mainly just sits at her desk flicking between Facebook and Twitter. Once, while presenting to a client, I popped my head out to ask her if she'd mind making coffees and she tweeted, "OMG, idiot at work just told me to make coffee. #imnotyourfuckingslave #spit."

I didn't see the tweet until after the presentation so I'm fairly sure I drank coffee with spit in it.

....

From: Jennifer Haines
To: David Thorne
Subject: Melissa

David,

All staff recruitment is to be approved by the HR department. Under no circumstances do you have authority to offer anyone a position here. Melissa has zero experience, zero qualifications and zero knowledge of the position.

Furthermore, she is not your cousin and the entire story about her parents dying in a fire was fabricated. I've spoken to her and she knows nothing about it. She has been given a trial period but do not let this happen again.

Jennifer

....

The phone rang again.
"Ben wants to speak to you." said Melissa, "He's on line 3."
Click.

"Hurro? Mr Moshiyoto?" I said in an old Asian woman's voice as per procedure. I can't recall why Ben and I started doing this but it would be weird to start answering the phone normally now.
"Terrible," said Ben, "I could tell it was you. It sounded more like a Mexican man with emphysema than an Asian woman. Hey, I was just wondering, do you like the band Linkin Park?"

When a client is given a timeline for project completion of, say, three weeks, this does not mean the project takes three weeks to complete. It means somewhere between looking at photos of cabbages, closing bathroom doors, discussing weapons of choice during a zombie apocalypse, answering phone calls, making your own coffee and drawing flags, a few hours will be spent quickly throwing their project together.

Often those few hours will be allocated to the few hours before the client arrives to view what you have been working on for three weeks.

I once designed a logo while a client waited in the foyer. Melissa entertained them with an explanation of why she chose to wear boots with leggings rather than boots with a dress that day while I turned an 8 sideways to make an infinity symbol, chopped a bit out of one of the loops, and turned it orange. The new logo was presented ten minutes later to the client, a large financial investment company, as "a graphic representation of koi which are symbolic of wealth in Japanese culture."

"It's beautiful. Simple yet balanced, solid yet flowing. I also love the typeface you used for our name, what's it called?"
"Helvetica."
"Just stunning."

A few years before, while working for an Australian design agency called De Masi Jones, I was commissioned to come up with a new name and branding for a flight training company. Forgetting about the project until the day due, they were presented with the name 'Altara' and told it was an aboriginal word, from the Boonjari tribe, meaning 'above the clouds'. The client was happy and Altara is now an established brand in the aeronautics industry. There is no such thing as the Boonjari tribe.

While it is entirely possible that spending time allocated to a project on the actual project might produce a better result, it's a scenario I have no experience with or expectations of.

"We charged the client for 132 hours, how many hours were spent?"
"132"
"Oh no, what happened? We will never make money like that."
"I'm kidding, it was 2."
"Thank god. By the way, have I shown you my new golf clubs? I'll bring them upstairs to your office and demonstrate club selection, stance, swing and follow-through even though you have no interest in the subject. Kevin, would you like to join me? While I'm setting up a makeshift putting green, you can explain to David the importance of good soil drainage."

Kevin returned a short time later and made his way into my office.
"The spears look better," he commented, "one's a bit bent though. It wouldn't be very aerodynamic."
"What can I help you with, Kevin?"
"I just want to show you something," he replied, taking out his iPhone.
"Fantastic, I hope it's a photo of cabbage."
"Look... no, that's not... here it is!"
The photo showed Kevin, down on one knee, holding a measuring tape across the top of a cabbage.

"Eleven and a half inches," he proclaimed proudly, "The key is making sure the soil has a pH balance between 6.5 and 7.5."

Copywriters

I saw a show on television recently in which a man wearing a green John Deere cap rolled his dead coworker up in a rug and threw him off a bridge. I came in late to the program so I have no idea how either of them came to be in this situation but I assume they fought over corn or something.

The rug was nice, white with a subtle chequered pattern, and I thought it highly unlikely that someone who wears a John Deere cap would own a contemporary rug like that. People who wear John Deere caps prefer ornate things. A contemporary rug wouldn't go with their green velour couch or the maple and glass cabinet containing ceramic horse figurines. An Oriental or Persian looking rug would make more sense. It wouldn't show the dirt as much. I looked online and found the exact white chequered rug at IKEA for $299 so I ordered it. People who wear John Deere caps don't shop online, or at IKEA, they shop at Grande Home Furnishings & Mattresses.

The man wearing a green John Deere cap was apprehended fairly quickly as the contemporary rug was discovered the next morning with his fingerprints all over the rubber backing. His prints were on file as he had a prior arrest for stealing three rolls of fencing wire from the back of a hardware store. If I ever have to roll a coworker up in a rug and throw him off a bridge, I will remember to roll him up with the carpeted side facing outwards. I will also take a flashlight with me to check if the creek has any water in it. Also, if I regularly wore a green John Deere cap, I would swap it out for the occassion, perhaps with a beanie, just in case a homeless person living under the bridge later agrees to serve as witness for the prosecution.

I rolled up our new IKEA rug a few days ago and took it down to the basement. One of our dogs took a huge dump on it and I couldn't get out the stain. I tried moving the furniture around to hide it but wasn't happy with the layout. The rug was pretty heavy. I had to drag it most of the way and needed a nap afterwards. The man wearing a green John Deere cap must have been a lot stronger than me, probably from years of lifting pigs and polishing his tractor, as there's no way I'd manage to lift a rug over a railing if it included a body.

A better solution might be to strap the rug to the roof of your car and park really close to the edge so it can be rolled off - or, keep the rug, especially if it's a nice one, drive the dead coworker out into a forested area, or a park if you live in the city, and sit them against a tree with a compass in one hand and a map of a completely different area in the other. This way it would appear they simply got lost while hiking and did not posess the necessary survival skills to find their way out. You could leave a bag of trail mix with only the bits nobody likes left in their pocket to allay suspicion.

If the coworker is known to enjoy hiking, people will say, "Oh yes, he often went hiking, at least he died doing what he loved," and if he is not the type to go hiking, it will explain why he was so bad at it. Before leaving the office and heading out to the forested area, you could use his computer to send the secretary an email stating, "I'm completely out of pens. Could I have one of the nice Pilot ones and a couple of Bics from the supply cabinet please? Also, I'm going for a hike." To prevent this ever happening to me, I tell everyone in the office once a day that I have no interest whatsoever in hiking.

I've been hiking. It was recently and it was dreadful. There were steep hills, bushes with barbs, and spiders. These are things I usually go out of my way to avoid. Every four or five steps I walked into webs stretched across trees and most of them housed spiders that looked like mushrooms with legs. After the first few dozen, I made my hiking companion Ben - a copywriter I worked with that had convinced me to join him through deceptive descriptions of light-dappled paths beside streams - walk ahead of me.

I saw a documentary years ago about a six-year-old child with a medical condition called Progeria that aged him faster than normal. His skin looked like a Spacesaver bag with the air sucked out and while he was talking to the camera about his favourite toy, a Buzz Lightyear action figure with flick-out wings, one of his teeth fell out. He was short and skinny and had a huge wrinkly head shaped like a potato.

I'd asked Ben many times if he had this condition but he said he didn't.

"I haven't walked into any spider webs," he declared after a short time. This was due to Ben's small proportions while the spiders, seemingly on purpose, hung at normal human level. I tried convincing him to puff up his beanie like a gnome's hat but he refused stating, "that's not how beanies are worn," and, "there could be other hikers on the path and I might forget to flatten my beanie back down before they see me."

As such, I spent the next several miles waving a stick frantically in front of me before each step. If I hadn't been so pre-occupied with waving a stick, I might have noticed the deep muddy hole. Miserably swishing my stick and describing to Ben all the things I would rather be doing than hiking, my left leg suddenly disappeared to the knee. Jolted sideways, my upper half fell into a bush that combined all the joys of hiking by featuring not only barbs, but several webs and spiders and one of those weird sack things that looks a bit like a spider web but is full of hundreds of little worms. The next few seconds were a blur but included screaming.

Reaching out for Ben, expecting his hand to be there waiting, I stared down the path to see him shaking his head as he disappeared around a bend.

"Ben!" I yelled. No reply. "BEN!"

Under no delusion of possessing the necessary survival skills to find my way should Ben get too far ahead of me, I pivoted into an uprightish position and, with a huge slurping noise, managed to pull my leg free. As my calf and foot were now surrounded by several inches of blackish sludge, it took me a moment to realise that my boot had stayed behind.

I was a bit upset by this as I'd purchased the boots a few days before from Zappo's specifically for the occassion. They sent me brown ones instead of the black ones I ordered and I didn't have time to return them so I'd spent a good couple of hours colouring them in with a Sharpie the night before. As far as I was concerned, this was the end of the hike and we would probably have to be rescued.

I poked the muddy hole a few times with my spider stick, which produced no result, then chased after Ben with a kind of 'big step, little step' gait while waving my stick in front. Rather than the thick mud around my foot falling off, or at least providing some form of protection from dirt and rocks on the path, the dirt and rocks adhered to the mud, forming a large conglomerate of misery.

"Ben," I yelled, cupping my free hand around my mouth because that's how you yell in the forest, "I lost my boot. Wait."

Rounding the bend, I discovered Ben sitting cross-legged on a rock, sipping from a tube that went over his shoulder into his backpack. He was obviously going for the 'one with nature' thing but looked more like the weird worm thing from *Alice in Wonderland* that sits on a mushroom. I told him this.

"Look," I also declared, indicating the mass surrounding my foot, "what are we going to do?"
"Take your sock off," Ben replied.
This was sound advice so I argued against it for a bit before peeling it off.
"How much longer before we get to the car?" I craned my neck to peer up the path hopefully.
"What do you mean? It depends on when we stop and turn back."

I had, up until that point, assumed we were walking on some kind of loop that would eventually take us back to our starting point. Which is the problem with copywriters. They leave out important information and fill the void with lies about light-dappled paths beside streams.

This deception is not constrained to forest-based activities either. A few weeks prior to the hike, Ben tricked me into attending a party at his house by stating it would be fun and full of interesting people. Instead, Ben's girlfriend gave a half hour presentation about something called Herbalife to Ben, myself, and Ben's parents.

I was home, with a large tub of protein-shake mix, in time to watch *The Bachelor*. I must have misunderstood part of the presentation because each month for the next year, I received a new tub of protein-shake mix, an invoice for forty-eight dollars, and instructions on how to hold my own Herbalife parties.

Also, I once tried on Ben's black-rimmed glasses, to see how bad his eyesight was, and the lenses had zero magnification.

Which, I suppose, is no different from styling your hair a certain way or wearing attire that presents to others who you want to be. When I was eight, I wore a scarf for almost a year, regardless of the temperature, because someone told me it looked Bohemian. I had no idea what Bohemian meant but I knew it had something to do with the band Queen and the movie Flash Gordon was very popular at the time.

You only have to enter a Walmart in Virginia to experience what the world would be like if everyone stopped caring.

"Look Evelyn, *Duck Dynasty* wiper blades. We should get them."

I recently visited a Walmart at 2am with my fifteen-year-old offspring Seb to purchase paintball gun ammunition. On the way back to our vehicle, an elderly lady wearing a nightie asked politely if we wanted to buy a cat. She had a whole box of them.

Seb peered into the box looking worried, "Are they alive?"
The lady rummaged in the box for a bit and held one up,
"This one is," she said.

Seb drove to Walmart that night. He wasn't legally allowed
to operate a motor vehicle yet but I'd let him drive around
the block a few times and once to the hardware store to
practice. We live in a small village an hour or so from D.C.
and the term 'peak hour traffic' refers to there being more
tractors on the road than usual.

"Hey Seb, remember that time you rubbed poo on the walls?
You were two."
"No."
"Well you did. All four walls of your bedroom. It was
disgusting. Watch out for the tree."
"What tree?"
"All the trees. Being alert of all possible hazards, immediate
and pending, is the key to being a good driver."
"The tree isn't going to jump out onto the road. Telling me
to watch out for things that I don't have to watch out for is
just distracting."
"Fine. Watch out for that wheelie bin."
"Dad."
"It was sticking out from the curb a bit."
"Not really."
"Yes it was. It could have *wheelie bin* dangerous."
"Hmm."
"Get it? *Wheelie bin* dangerous."

"Yes, I get it. It just wasn't very funny."

"Yes it was. I love you so much."

"What?"

"I said I love you so much."

"Okay."

"And I'm very proud of you."

"Why are you telling me this? Are you dying?"

"No, if I was dying you'd know about it. I'd milk the sympathy to the last drop. I'm just feeling a bit sentimental. It seems like only yesterday you were rubbing poo on walls and now you're driving. I'll blink and you will have kids of your own. I hope they rub poo on your walls. Then *you* will blink and they will be driving. It's the circle of life. Like in *The Lion King*."

"Not really."

"Yes it is. I'm the dad lion, what's his name, Mufasa? And you're that other one."

"Simba."

"No, what's the warthog's name?"

"Pumbaa?"

"That's the one. One moment Pumbaa Junior will be rubbing poo on your walls and the next, you'll be letting him drive to Walmart. Try to remember the wheelie bin joke for when that happens."

The purpose for the 2am excursion was that I'd agreed to participate in a paintball match the next day with a coworker named Simon and while up late researching the topic, I'd read that if you put the paintballs in the freezer overnight, they hurt a lot more. As it turned out, Simon and I were placed on the same team but that just made it easier to get a clean shot.

For those that have never played Paintball, it is exactly like those mediaeval gatherings where a group of people named Timothy and Geoffrey don chainmail and rush at each-other in the forest with wooden swords for king and honour. Except with guns that shoot things that look like those little balls you put in the bath. The ones that dissolve and make the water smell nice that generally come with a bar of soap in a little wicker basket wrapped in cellophane that people you couldn't care less about are given as Christmas presents. I received one last year as my staff 'Secret Santa' present and it still had a little tag attached with gold ribbon that read, "To Sarah, Merry Xmas 04." This annoyed me somewhat as I had actually put some thought into my gift. Louise, who is quite fat, seemed quite overwhelmed with her trial subscription to Weight Watchers Online.

I attended a mediaeval gathering once but only because my friend Geoffrey needed a lift. People who participate in mediaeval gatherings don't tend to own vehicles. I sat in my car the entire time to avoid being asked, "Whateth is this strange garb thou weareth?"

Adding 'eth' to the end of a word doesn't make it mediaeval, it makes it stupid. After about an hour of watching Geoffrey leap out from behind trees and whack people with his sword,

I wound down the window and yelled, "How long are you going to be Geoffrey?" and he yelled back, "That's *Sir* Geoffrey, my goodeth fellow."

I'm fairly certain nobody in mediaeval times said the word 'goodeth' and there is no way Geoffrey would have been a knight if he'd been born in mediaeval times. He'd be the one being whacked by knights for not growing enough potatoes and making up words. After a hard day's work and several whackings, he'd lay down in the soil, cover himself with straw, and go to sleep imagining all the things he would do to the knights if he were a wizard.

All to their own though. Some people like to pretend they are knights or soldiers or wizards and some people like to pretend they need glasses. Or a beanie in the middle of summer.

"There's no way I'm giving you my beanie to wear on your foot," said Ben.
"I need it," I explained, "I can't walk all the way back like this. Not with only one boot. I could tie it on with one of your shoelaces. Take some responsibility, if you'd have asked me if I wanted to spend the day walking through hundreds of spider webs and falling into bogs instead of making it out to be something not horrible, I wouldn't be here."

It wasn't even a nice beanie, if there is such a thing. It was grey, with thin green stripes, and the way he wore it with the saggy end hanging loose and rippled at the back made it look like a giant grub was eating his head.

I'm not a huge fan of beanies. Whenever I try one on, I look like I should be casting nets over the side of a fishing trawler. I only ever wear one when I am snowboarding and even then I can tell everyone is wondering what I am doing so far from my ship.

"Why are you even wearing a beanie?" I asked, "Is there a fishing village further up the trail?"
"It keeps the ticks out of my hair," Ben replied.
"The what?"
He reached out and picked something off my neck, holding it up for me to see. "The ticks."
"Oh my god."
"You've got another one on your forehead."

Having lived in cities most of my life, I'd never seen a real tick before that moment but years earlier I'd read a news article online, with accompanying graphic photos, of someone who had a tick on their eyeball. It had burrowed its way in fairly well.

I frantically ran my hands over my face and through my hair and ripped off my shirt. I don't tend to take my shirt off in public, not even at the beach, so when I do, it looks like I am wearing a tight white t-shirt with nipple and a navel graphics. Against the stark background of my chest and stomach, the eleven ticks stood out like dog turds on a new IKEA rug.

"Are there any in my eyes?" I screamed, holding them open and thrusting my face forward for inspection.

Which is when another two hikers walked around the bend. They paused, took in the situation, then proceeded to pass silently while avoiding eye contact.

"I've got ticks," I called after them as explanation.

"Just so you know," said Ben as he started back the way we had come, "this is the worst hike I have ever been on."
"Well yes, I suppose it would have to be," I agreed, "If it was as dreadful as this every time you'd have to be insane to do it twice."
"No, I meant hiking with you."

Copywriting basically consists of taking something dreadful, putting it in a box with a shiny ribbon, and presenting it to someone. Any disappointment the recipient has upon opening the box is entirely due to their own high expectations and therefore their fault.

"Oh no, the box is full of spiders!"
"And? Your disappointment is entirely due to your own high expectations."
"You told me it was a puppy."

I once ordered a set of 'Japanese Garden Lanterns' online that had the description, "A centuries-old artform, these traditional Japanese lanterns are sure to take pride of place in any garden or patio setting. Add a touch of the exotic to your outdoor lifestyle." I received a foot-long string of lights, powered by a single AAA battery, with four plastic lanterns each an inch in diameter. There was meant to be five lanterns but one of the LED's was missing one. I doubt very much that Japanese people living centuries ago invited guests out to their garden to show off their foot long string of plastic lanterns.

"They're beautiful Mr Yamaha, but is that LED missing a lantern?"
"Yes, I should probably wrap a bit of electrical tape around that LED so it isn't so obvious."

I wrapped a bit of electrical tape around the bare LED so it wasn't so obvious and hung the string of lanterns outside on a branch. It wasn't long enough to reach another branch so it hung vertically. Rather than adding a touch of the exotic to my outdoor lifestyle, it added a fair degree of disappointment. After a few days, I hid it in a kitchen drawer. I should probably have returned it but that would have entailed printing out a shipping label or something.

The house to our right has approximately forty Japanese lanterns hanging in a meticulously sculptured Asian-inspired yard. Every time I glance in their direction, it's as if the lanterns are saying, "Lol, you should have read the product specifications," and sometimes, "Steal us."

If I did steal them, I would have to hang them inside with the blinds permanently drawn but if I replaced all my furniture with a large rock and had sand brought in, it would add more than a touch of the exotic to my indoor lifestyle and I wouldn't have to worry about poo on rugs. Visitors could draw concentric rings in the sand around the rock while I played them a song with my Kokorikok sticks.
"Your koi are getting large," they'd say.
"Yes," I'd reply, gazing down from my little wooden bridge, "I changed their food to a high protein mix recently that includes red krill. It costs a little more but they seem to like it. Any requests?"
"Play the one that goes 'clack, clack, click, clack'. That's my favourite."

In Australia, jumping a fence and taking things from your neighbour's yard is a generally accepted practice known as 'Snow Dropping'. While the term covers potted plants, hose fittings and garden furniture, it mainly refers to clothing. Due to the warm climate, most Australians hang their washing outside on a clothesline overnight to dry. This cuts down on the costs of running a dryer and the savings can be put towards purchasing new clothes when you find yours missing in the morning. It is not uncommon to be driving through your suburb a few days later and see a neighbour mowing his lawn in your favourite jeans and t-shirt. With your lawn-mower.

I'm not sure why it is called Snow Dropping but giving a cute sounding name to a shitty act somehow makes it more acceptable. A copywriter probably came up with it.

"We love the new name, do you have anything to replace the term 'child abuse'?"
"How about Snuggle Booping?"
"Perfect. Anything for 'pointless travel involving spiders and ticks'?"
"Hmm, how about Clompily Plomping?"
"No, that sounds stupid, you're just making words up now."

The word 'hike' originally comes from the time when the husband would ride on a mule while the wife had to walk alongside. As the routes were unpaved and muddy, the wife would have to 'hike up her skirt'. If she complained, the husband was allowed to hit her with a stick.

Women in the seventeenth century probably regarded the question, "Who's up for a hike?" with the same horror I now do.

If I lived in the seventeenth century, I wouldn't hit my wife with a stick or make her walk alongside my mule. I'd give her the stick and make her walk in front, waving it about to make sure there weren't any webs. It can't be that difficult to hike up your dress with one hand.

"I recognise that tree stump," I told Ben, "It's where you ate the Clif Bar."

I'd sampled a small piece and it tasted like a little brick of sadness.

Ben grunted. He hadn't said much on the return journey.

"That means only a few miles of sharp rocks to go," I added in what I thought was an enthusiastic manner. Ben grunted again.

"I'm sorry about your beanie."

There had been a minor scuffle a few miles earlier.

"You could probably stitch it back up and nobody would notice."

Nothing.

"If you used the same colour thread it..."

Ben grabbed the beanie from his head and threw it into the forest. It might have been more dramatic had the angle of the throw not caused the beanie to catch air, like a frisbee thrown almost straight up, and return to land a few feet from where we were standing.

"That was lucky," I said, slipping my bare foot into it.

Ben stared. "If I killed you out here, nobody would discover the body for ages. By that time, forest animals would have eaten most of you."

"They'd have to beat the ticks to it," I replied, "Besides, the hikers that passed us will eventually work out that they are not on a loop and come back this way. You'd have to quickly hide my body off the path and I doubt you'd be able to lift me, what with your Progeria."

"I don't have Progeria," Ben lied, "and I wouldn't have to lift you. I'd get you to leave the path with me and *then* I'd kill you."

"And how exactly would you make me leave the path?"

"I wouldn't have to *make* you. I know you like frogs so I'd say 'there's a pond just off the path up here, last time I looked it had about a hundred frogs. One was orange with white spots. Do you want to have a quick look?' and you'd *want* to leave the path."

I do like frogs but I don't wear t-shirts with pictures of frogs on them or collect frog trading cards. It's more of a, "oh look, a frog," kind of thing. I would be more impressed by an orange frog with white spots but I'd probably still say "oh look, a frog." Just quicker with a tinge of wonder. Regardless, I don't believe I had ever mentioned frogs to Ben.

"When did I say I like frogs?" I asked.

"It's not about frogs, that was just an example, it's about making you want to do something, not making you do something."

"You'd be better off saying it's a shortcut back to the car," I replied, "The bit about the orange frog with white spots was pretty good though."

"Thanks. There actually is a short cut up here though, do you want to take it?"

"No."

A couple of weeks later, Ben asked me if I liked the band Linkin Park. He had an extra concert ticket to "a really amazing band I think you'll also like" who were playing that night. The band's name, The Calling, should probably have been a red flag but I only realised something was awry after Ben and his girlfriend picked me up from my house. He was wearing a white shirt, slacks and leather business slippers, while his girlfriend was wearing an ankle length floral dress with some kind of weird doily thing around the neck. The concert was at their church and Ben's dad was the bass guitarist. The audience totalled maybe thirty people.

"They're up late," I said to Ben nodding towards his siblings. The youngest was four and also dressed in shirt, slacks and leather business slippers. I'd worn a red Pop Will Eat Itself tour t-shirt with the words *Sample it, loop it, fuck it, eat it, and spit it out!* written across the front. Ben's mother gave me a Band-Aid to put over the word fuck. Ben's grandmother was parked in the aisle next to me. She was paralysed from the neck down due to a severe stroke but could control her wheelchair with a rubber thing that went in her mouth. Whenever she had something to say, she'd pucker her lips around the control, rotate towards me, and mumble something unintelligible before rotating back.
"What did she say?" asked Ben, leaning over.
"I'm not sure, but it might have been, 'Please kill me'," I replied.
The band finished playing Proud Mary and Ben's dad approached the microphone.

"We're going to take a quick five minute break now as Dennis has a cramp. Please help yourself to refreshments and chips in the foyer."

"You told me the band was like Linkin Park," I said to Ben.

"No," he replied, "I only asked if you liked them."

Badminton

I died when I was ten. I stopped breathing and my heart stopped beating. My father didn't know CPR but he tried blowing into my mouth and hitting my chest while my mother, grandparents, sister and cousins stood in a ring around me waiting for the ambulance to arrive.

I had a dream while I was dead. I was swimming and the water turned to ice around me. There weren't any lights or tunnels like I have heard other people describe, just ice. I could see my arms below the surface but I couldn't move them. My legs were also trapped but the frozen layer stopped at my ankles, leaving my feet free to move in the water below. I saw a large dark shape swimming under me. It brushed my left foot.
"David!"
There was suddenly a lot of noise. Sirens, yelling, beeping.
"He's conscious."

Badminton is a stupid game and people look stupid while they are playing it. My cousin Susan, a large girl, played competitive badminton for a team. Who plays badminton for a team? It's a game for backyards and bored children. She and I were playing against each other at her house during a family gathering. The adults were inside eating fondue and listening to Boney-M records.

I'd never played badminton before and the fact that Susan was losing by several points was making her quite upset. She blamed the wind direction, and her shoes, and how spongy the grass was. I suggested it might be because the game is easy and stupid and not a real sport like tennis.

"Of course it's a real sport. What would you know?"
"I know I'm winning even though I've never played before."
"Only because this isn't my regular racquet."
"This isn't my regular racquet either."
"I'm actually just letting you win. I usually play really well. I've got a trophy."
"Really? For badminton or pie eating?"

My sister and I were under strict instructions never to mention Susan's weight. We'd been told that she had a medical condition or something but every time I saw her, she had a mouth full of chips, cake or sausage. It wasn't just 'big bones', she had no neck. She looked like a slug, with other slugs for legs and arms.

Susan lost it. She kicked over one of the poles that was holding up the badminton net and threw her racquet into the air. It landed on the roof of the house. She glared at me, gave me the finger, and stormed inside.

My sister had been waiting to play the winner and groaned about the loss of the racquet.
"You"ll have to go up there and get it," she said.

"I'm not going up there," I replied. It was a double story house.

"Oh, go on. If you climb on to the water tank, you should be able to reach that tree branch which goes up to the roof. It looks easy."

"You do it then."

"I'm wearing sandals."

"Fine."

As champion of the game and having nothing else to do, I was kind of keen to play again. Making it up *was* actually easy. I stepped from the branch onto the roof and edged my way along the slope to the racquet.

I heard the front door slam. "Where's David?" yelled my father. My sister pointed. He craned his head around and up.

"What the fuck are you doing up there?"

I held the racquet up to show him.

"Did you call Susan fat?"

"No, she said she had a trophy and I asked if it was for eating pies."

"Right, you're in big fucking trouble. Get down here now. You're going to go in there and apologise to her in front of everybody."

"No."

I'd have spent the rest of my life on the roof rather than face the humiliation of apologising in front of everybody.

"Don't make me come up there."

I sat down.

It had taken me about three minutes to get up, it took him less than one. He was also wearing sandals so I call bullshit on my sister's excuse. I panicked, looking for another way down as he stepped off the branch. There was a concrete driveway below me but on the other side of that was a garage. I decided, given enough run-up, I would be able to make it. From there, it would be a simple task to drop onto the neighbouring property fence and escape through their yard. My father edged along the sloping roof towards me. I backed up a bit, ran, and jumped. I mostly blame the incline as you need a flat area for a decent run up. Also, as I stepped on the edge of the roof and leapt, the gutter gave way, cancelling any propulsion upwards. I flailed. I have a vague recollection of what concrete looks like as it rushes towards you at high speed but I don't remember the impact.

"David, can you tell me how old you are?"
"nnn."
"Can you try wiggling your fingers for me?"
"nnn nn."
"Ok, you're going to be fine. We're in an ambulance on the way to the hospital. Your Dad's here. Would you like him to sit with you?"
"nn o."

I was in surgery for eight hours and in hospital for three months. The right side of my skull had been fractured, shattered really, several fragments were removed from my brain. My collar bone, right arm, six ribs and left foot were also broken but brain trauma was the main concern. I forgot things. Not all things, just some things. Things like bath plugs and rabbits. I had all of my motor skills and could remember the name of every *Star Wars* character, but I had no idea what a blender was or what a round, orange coloured fruit was called. I knew the colour orange but there was a broken link somewhere. It didn't concern me that much, I understood that I had forgotten things but I had no idea what things they were until I came across them and then it was just as if I had never known about that particular thing in the first place.

"What's this thing? Is it a belt?"
"No, it's called a leash. It connects to a dog's collar so you can take the dog for a walk without it running away."
"Clever."

A man with a grey beard and blue glasses visited me regularly in the hospital to play games. His name was Henry. The games mainly consisted of naming the item pictured on cards he held up. He'd pause often and scribble in a notebook. Sometimes he would sing parts of songs and ask me to finish them.

"Bathroom tiles?"
"Okay. What else is white?"
"The lamb?"
"Well yes, but you wouldn't say Mary's lamb is as white as the lamb. What else could a lamb be as white as? Something

white and cold..."
"A glass of milk?"

For the first few weeks, I shared a room with another boy my age named Mark. He only had one arm. Apparently he had opened a top loading washing machine lid while it was in spin cycle and reached in to grab an item of clothing. His arm was twisted off at the shoulder. Sometimes when Henry would ask me a question or hold up a picture, Mark would answer for me and say things like, "Oh my god, I can't believe you don't know what a turtle is. Everybody knows what a turtle is," so Henry moved me to a different room by myself.

It was a smaller room, white with no window or television. There was a painting on the wall of a beach at sunset but Henry took it down. I read a lot of books. There wasn't anything else to do. Henry gave me a highlighter pen and asked me to mark any words I came across that I didn't know but it was easy to cheat by looking up the words in a dictionary.

Sometimes when Henry visited, he was accompanied by three or four other people. While Henry and I played games, they stood in a corner watching. Occasionally he would ask them a question and there would be a discussion about things such as ventral streams and parietal lobes. The term Agnosia was used a lot.

"Snow."

"Very good. And can you describe snow for me?"

"Frozen water crystals that fall if the temperature is low enough. It's fluffy and white. Like lamb fleece."

"And can you tell me what this is a picture of?"

"A turtle."

My parents took me home. Every few weeks I met with Henry for an hour or so but these meetings eventually became shorter and less frequent. I returned to school. Over the next few years, occasions where I would hear a word or discover an item that was new to me became less constant - perhaps once a month - but again, I wasn't to know if I had always not known them.

It came in handy sometimes. I would pretend not to know what a vacuum cleaner or lawn mower was. Before the accident, I used to get dropped off at my piano teacher's house ever Thursday night for an hour. Her name was Mrs Williams. For the first half-hour she would yell at me for not practicing then spend the rest of the time talking about her fourteen cats. I had no idea what I was even meant to be learning. She said I was the worst student she had ever had. Sometimes she would call me Dennis and make me fix stuff around the house. Once, she made me run a bath and help her in. I would have told my parents but they might have made me go to a different teacher and then I would have had to learn to play the piano. After the accident, I just pretended to not know what a piano was.

I hadn't lost ten years of things. Just things dotted amongst that ten years. It didn't take ten years to reknow these things either, if I had ever known them. From age ten and up it is easier to grasp things than it is at four or five. I eventually stopped playing 'did I know this?' with myself. Like everyone else, there were just things I know, things I have never known, and things I have forgotten. I may have once known what a Lychee is but it doesn't matter. I'm not going to buy one anyway.

My son received a badminton set from his auntie on his tenth birthday. Neither of us had ever heard of badminton but we read the rules and put up the net on our back lawn. We hit a floaty thing with skinny racquets for fifteen minutes and became bored. It was easy and stupid and not a real sport like tennis.

Interviews

A few weeks ago, the company I work for lost a designer. While in the middle of a client meeting - explaining to a rep from Kraft Foods why fourteen pages of text cannot fit on the back of 320mL jar label - Simon stood, stated, "I can't do this anymore," and left. His dramatic exit scene was diminished somewhat when, despite having opened and closed the board room door hundreds of times before, he pulled and shook the handle for several seconds yelling, "what the fuck is wrong with this door?" before remembering it swung outwards.

Earlier that week, Simon had confided to Melissa that he was having 'relationship issues' so everyone knew within an hour that his girlfriend had slept with a white-water rafting instructor.

Simon's father came in to collect his personal belongings a few days later and when I asked how Simon was doing, he replied, "He'll be fine, what doesn't kill you makes you stronger." Which isn't always true as I know someone who contracted Ross River Virus several years ago and he needs to be pushed around in a wheel-chair, moaning the whole time about his joints and inadequate ramp access. I visited him in his ground-floor apartment once but it was a miserable and forced conversation so I told him I had a present for him in the car and went to get it. Then drove home.

....

From: Mike Campbell
Date: Wednesday 4 June 2014 10.09am
To: David Thorne
Subject: Job interviews

David,

My flight is at 2pm today but I need to pack so I'll leave around 12. I fly back Tuesday morning. Jennifer is on annual leave so you and Kevin will have to hold the first round of interviews for the new designer in my absence. Please rearrange your schedule for Thursday and Friday to suit.

The resumes are on my desk in the blue folder. There are 7 interviews on Thursday and 6 on Friday. Ask Melissa to make sure the board room is clean and offer applicants coffee when they arrive. We're only selecting 5 for final interviews so let's get a good feel for fit. Please organize a list of 10 questions for the applicants before tomorrow and attach their answers to the top of each resume so I can go through them next week. What are their strengths and weaknesses? Are they proactive or reactive? etc.

Mike

From: David Thorne
Date: Wednesday 4 June 2014 10.26am
To: Mike Campbell
Subject: Re: Job interviews

Mike,

No problem. I will perform a Google search for 'modern interviewing techniques circa 1982' right away. The importance of determining which applicants are capable of providing contrived responses to stupid questions cannot be overstated. It is essentially the key to getting on well with everyone here.

It's possible, however, more could be learned, and a greater 'feel for fit' obtained, through open discussion. Perhaps over a beer.

I therefore suggest Kevin and I meet each applicant in the board room before proceeding to the local bar to chat. Or wait there and have Melissa give them directions.

David

From : Mike Campbell
Date : Wednesday 4 June 2014 10.55am
To : David Thorne
Subject : Re: Re: Job interviews

David,

All interviews will take place in the board room. Asking set questions means I can rate the answers when I get back. What will I have to go on if you just chat?

It's going to be a busy month and we need to replace Simon immediately. With someone normal. The questions will help us avoid a repeat of last month's embarrassing drama. I'm sorry he's having issues but people need to learn to leave their personal lives at the door. This isn't the Kardashians.

Mike

....

From : David Thorne
Date : Wednesday 4 June 2014 11.18am
To : Mike Campbell
Subject : Re: Re: Re: Job interviews

Mike,

I'm not sure what *Star Trek* has to do with any of this but embarrassing drama is standard operating procedure around here. Bringing someone normal into the fold would just be cruel.

Melissa isn't speaking to anyone because she just found out Jennifer makes more than her and Jennifer has gone emergency hat shopping due to her hairdresser cutting her bangs too short. As she left, I heard Melissa say to someone on the phone, "It must be nice to be able to afford hats." I won't bother going into my own daily drama, but I'm fairly positive you're not going to like it. Kevin is the only 'normal' person here and that's because he gave up on having a personality when he discovered gardening. Nobody cares how your cabbages are doing, Kevin.

But yes, it is certainly possible that had Simon been asked what his weakness is prior to employment, that particular drama may have been avoided. When selecting final candidates from this week's interviews, we will immediately weed out those answering, "Dramatic things might happen during a client meeting if I ever find out my partner had sex with a white-water rafting instructor while away on holiday for three days."

Do we also discard the likes of, "If I ever go hiking on the edge of a volcano I might slip and fall into lava without backing up my work," or do these go in the 'maybe' pile with, "I've been known to get caught in open fields during lightning storms"?

Multiple-choice questions might streamline the process. This would provide a range of possible scenarios to preempt and serve as a score tally to go on. Should there be a draw, we can have the finalists guess the amount of jellybeans in a jar, and time how long it takes them to do twenty push-ups for bonus points. Any remaining interview time that would otherwise be wasted on chatting can be spent quietly avoiding eye contact.

In addition to those already suggested, are there any specific pointless questions you want included?

David

....

From : Mike Campbell
Date : Wednesday 4 June 2014 11.41am
To : David Thorne
Subject : Re: Re: Re: Re: Job interviews

How is this an issue?

Just ask 10 fucking interview questions. I don't care what they are as long as I have a record. And add notes so you can remember who they are.

Mike

Applicant Questionnaire

Name *Michelle Roper*

Day of Interview ☑Thursday ☐ Friday | **Time of Interview** *4 pm*

---

1 How is this an issue?   *" It isn't. Go ahead."*

---

2 To evaluate strengths & weaknesses, please rate your chance of survival in the following situations:

Slipping on a rock, possibly while hiking, and falling into lava. *0* %

Building an enlargement ray and testing it on a flower but a bee gets caught in the beam and turns to the size of a bus and stings you in the face. *20* %

Being kidnapped while back-packing across Europe and having a German scientist sew your mouth onto the rectum of another back-packer. *10* %

Taking several rattlesnake bites to the neck. *0* %

Exploding. Note, you are not wearing safety glasses at the time. *0* %

---

3 Have you ever been caught in an open field during a lightning storm? ☐ Yes ☑No

If yes, were you holding a shovel? ☐ Yes ☐ No

---

4 Are you Proactive or Reactive? ☑Yes ☐No

---

5 Has your partner ever shown an interest in white-water rafting? ☐ Yes ☑No

---

6 Have you ever thought about what you would 'invent' to survive and prosper if you fell through a time portal and found yourself in Medieval England during the 11th century? ☑Yes ☐No

---

7 If you could be any member of the Kardassian family, which one would you choose?

☐ Willis   ☐ Arnold   ☑Kimberly   ☐ Mr Huxtable

---

8 Have you ever considered growing your own cabbage? ☐ Yes ☑No

---

9 There is a type of parasite that takes control of an ant's brain and makes it climb a blade of grass to wait for a hungry cow. The parasite then reproduces in the cow's lower intestine. When the cow drops its faeces, the parasites wait for ants to approach and the circle continues. Working in the design & advertising industry is most like being:

☐ The Ant
☐ The Cow
☑ The Parasite
☐ The Faeces

---

10 If you knew a spell to summon Jesus, what would you use your one wish for?

☑Infinite wishes   ☐ A new car   ☐ To be an eagle   ☐ Cake

Additional Notes
Short lesbian wearing a Blondie t-shirt.
Excellent portfolio.   ★Recommend for
Good communication.   final interview. ★

Applicant Questionnaire

Name *Walton Bowers*

Day of Interview ☐ Thursday ☑ Friday   **Time of Interview** 2 : 00

---

1 How is this an issue?   *"Is that one of the questions?"*

---

2 To evaluate strengths & weaknesses, please rate your chance of survival in the following situations:

Slipping on a rock, possibly while hiking, and falling into lava. *30* %

Building an enlargement ray and testing it on a flower but a bee gets caught in the beam and turns to the size of a bus and stings you in the face. *30* %

Being kidnapped while back-packing across Europe and having a German scientist sew your mouth onto the rectum of another back-packer. *70* %

Taking several rattlesnake bites to the neck. *20* %

Exploding. Note, you are not wearing safety glasses at the time. *0* %

---

3 Have you ever been caught in an open field during a lightning storm? ☑ Yes ☐ No

If yes, were you holding a shovel? ☐ Yes ☑ No

---

4 Are you Proactive or Reactive? ☐ Yes ☑ No

---

5 Has your partner ever shown an interest in white-water rafting? ☐ Yes ☑ No

---

6 Have you ever thought about what you would 'invent' to survive and prosper if you fell through a time portal and found yourself in Mediaeval England during the 11th century? ☐ Yes ☑ No

---

7 If you could be any member of the Kardassian family, which one would you choose?

☐ Willis ☐ Arnold ☐ Kimberly ☑ Mr Huxtable

---

8 Have you ever considered growing your own cabbage? ☑ Yes ☐ No

---

9 There is a type of parasite that takes control of an ant's brain and makes it climb a blade of grass to wait for a hungry cow. The parasite then reproduces in the cow's lower intestine. When the cow drops its faeces, the parasites wait for ants to approach and the circle continues. Working in the design & advertising industry is most like being:

☑ The Ant
☐ The Cow
☐ The Parasite
☐ The Faeces

---

10 If you knew a spell to summon Jesus, what would you use your one wish for?

☐ Infinite wishes ☑ A new car ☐ To be an eagle ☐ Cake

Additional Notes

Came to interview wearing cargo shorts. Nice kid. Excellent portfolio - has worked on good projects. Talked to Kevin for 20 minutes about cabbages. *Recommend for final interview.*

Applicant Questionnaire

Name *Emily Bennett*

Day of Interview ☐ Thursday ☑ Friday   **Time of Interview** *11 AM*

---

1 How is this an issue? *"What? No, I was just scratching my nose."*

---

2 To evaluate strengths & weaknesses, please rate your chance of survival in the following situations:

Slipping on a rock, possibly while hiking, and falling into lava. __5__%

Building an enlargement ray and testing it on a flower but a bee gets caught in the beam and turns to the size of a bus and stings you in the face. __0__%

Being kidnapped while back-packing across Europe and having a German scientist sew your mouth onto the rectum of another back-packer. __0__%

Taking several rattlesnake bites to the neck. __10__%

Exploding. Note, you are not wearing safety glasses at the time. __0__%

---

3 Have you ever been caught in an open field during a lightning storm? ☐ Yes ☑ No

If yes, were you holding a shovel? ☐ Yes ☐ No

---

4 Are you Proactive or Reactive? ☑ Yes ☐ No

---

5 Has your partner ever shown an interest in white-water rafting? ☐ Yes ☑ No

---

6 Have you ever thought about what you would 'invent' to survive and prosper if you fell through a time portal and found yourself in Medieval England during the 11th century? ☐ Yes ☑ No

---

7 If you could be any member of the Kardassian family, which one would you choose?

☐ Willis ☐ Arnold ☑ Kimberly ☐ Mr Huxtable

---

8 Have you ever considered growing your own cabbage? ☑ Yes ☐ No

---

9 There is a type of parasite that takes control of an ant's brain and makes it climb a blade of grass to wait for a hungry cow. The parasite then reproduces in the cow's lower intestine. When the cow drops its faeces, the parasites wait for ants to approach and the circle continues. Working in the design & advertising industry is most like being:

☑ The Ant
☐ The Cow
☐ The Parasite
☐ The Faeces

---

10 If you knew a spell to summon Jesus, what would you use your one wish for?

☑ Infinite wishes ☐ A new car ☐ To be an eagle ☐ Cake

Additional Notes *Rode a bike to the interview. Parked it in the foyer so it wouldn't be stolen.*   **✳ Recommend for final interview.**

Solid portfolio. Very friendly and bright.

Applicant Questionnaire

Name Hoahan Nguyen

Day of Interview ☑Thursday ☐Friday **Time of Interview** / PM

1 How is this an issue? *"How is what an issue?"*

2 To evaluate strengths & weaknesses, please rate your chance of survival in the following situations:

Slipping on a rock, possibly while hiking, and falling into lava. __10__ %

Building an enlargement ray and testing it on a flower but a bee gets caught in the beam and turns to the size of a bus and stings you in the face. __0__ %

Being kidnapped while back-packing across Europe and having a German scientist sew your mouth onto the rectum of another back-packer. __15__ %

Taking several rattlesnake bites to the neck. __12__ %

Exploding. Note, you are not wearing safety glasses at the time. __0__ %

3 Have you ever been caught in an open field during a lightning storm? ☐Yes ☑No

If yes, were you holding a shovel? ☐Yes ☐No

4 Are you Proactive or Reactive? ☑Yes ☐No

5 Has your partner ever shown an interest in white-water rafting? ☐Yes ☑No

6 Have you ever thought about what you would 'invent' to survive and prosper if you fell through a time portal and found yourself in Medieaval England during the 11th century? ☐Yes ☑No

7 If you could be any member of the Kardassian family, which one would you choose?
☐Willis ☐Arnold ☑Kimberly ☐Mr Huxtable

8 Have you ever considered growing your own cabbage? ☐Yes ☑No

9 There is a type of parasite that takes control of an ant's brain and makes it climb a blade of grass to wait for a hungry cow. The parasite then reproduces in the cow's lower intestine. When the cow drops its faeces, the parasites wait for ants to approach and the circle continues. Working in the design & advertising industry is most like being:
☑The Ant
☐The Cow
☐The Parasite
☐The Faeces

10 If you knew a spell to summon Jesus, what would you use your one wish for?
☐Infinite wishes ☑A new car ☐To be an eagle ☐Cake

Additional Notes

Thin eyes. Possibly Asian.
Portfolio is exceptional - very clean design.
Good communication. ✳Recommend for final interview.

61

Applicant Questionnaire

Name *Wayne Redding*

| **Day of Interview** ☐ Thursday ☑ Friday | **Time of Interview** *10 AM* |

1 How is this an issue? *"I don't have an issue, I'm just nervous."*

2 To evaluate strengths & weaknesses, please rate your chance of survival in the following situations:

Slipping on a rock, possibly while hiking, and falling into lava. *10* %

Building an enlargement ray and testing it on a flower but a bee gets caught in the beam and turns to the size of a bus and stings you in the face. *50* %

Being kidnapped while back-packing across Europe and having a German scientist sew your mouth onto the rectum of another back-packer. *25* %

Taking several rattlesnake bites to the neck. *5* %

Exploding. Note, you are not wearing safety glasses at the time. *0* %

3 Have you ever been caught in an open field during a lightning storm? ☐ Yes ☑ No

If yes, were you holding a shovel? ☐ Yes ☐ No

4 Are you Proactive or Reactive? ☐ Yes ☐ No *"I don't follow politics."*

5 Has your partner ever shown an interest in white-water rafting? ☐ Yes ☑ No

6 Have you ever thought about what you would 'invent' to survive and prosper if you fell through a time portal and found yourself in Mediaeval England during the 11th century? ☑ Yes ☐ No

7 If you could be any member of the Kardassian family, which one would you choose?

☐ Willis ☑ Arnold ☐ Kimberly ☐ Mr Huxtable

8 Have you ever considered growing your own cabbage? ☐ Yes ☑ No

9 There is a type of parasite that takes control of an ant's brain and makes it climb a blade of grass to wait for a hungry cow. The parasite then reproduces in the cow's lower intestine. When the cow drops its faeces, the parasites wait for ants to approach and the circle continues. Working in the design & advertising industry is most like being:

☐ The Ant
☑ The Cow
☐ The Parasite
☐ The Faeces

10 If you knew a spell to summon Jesus, what would you use your one wish for?

☐ Infinite wishes ☑ A new car ☐ To be an eagle ☐ Cake

Additional Notes

Wayne was 15 minutes late and covered in sweat.
He missed the bus so ran here. In a suit.
Regardless, excellent portfolio. Nice kid.
Preds green tree frogs.
Recommend final interview.

From : Mike Campbell
Date : Tuesday 10 June 2014 12.21pm
To : David Thorne
Cc: Kevin Eastwood
Subject : No subject

David,

Can I see you and Kevin in my office please?

Mike

Woodwork

I visited Simon yesterday. He opened the front door of his small second floor apartment wearing pyjama pants and a stained *I heart LA* t-shirt. The apartment reeked of cigarette smoke and all the blinds were closed.

"What's up?" he asked.
"Nothing much," I replied, "Just checking in to make sure you haven't killed yourself. How are you doing?"
"Good."

Empty pizza boxes covered almost every inch of countertop and the sink was full of dishes. Little flies hovered above them. On a couch seat, next to a pillow and blanket, a pile of pizza crusts and cigarette butts had overflowed to the point where the ashtray had become a foundation rather than a container.

"Are you sleeping on the couch?" I asked.
"I'm not sleeping in *that* bed." Simon replied, sneering towards the bedroom he had, up until just a few weeks ago, shared with Cathy. "It smells like her."

I read the results of a poll once that showed 85% of married women have had an affair while holidaying without their partners. I'm sure it is a common occurrence, people being people, but you have to question how they come by these stats. I could ask a fisherman if he has gutted a fish lately and then state, "100% of all men polled say they have gutted a fish lately." The statement may be factual, but it is also construed.

I didn't know the whole story but according to office gossip, Simon's partner Cathy slept with a white-water rafting instructor while holidaying with her sister.

I've never been white-water rafting. Hurtling down a river in an inflatable boat with several other idiots - high-fiving each other the whole time and saying things like 'woo' - is on my reverse bucket-list of stupid things to avoid along with marathons, musical theatre and lip piercings.

"Let's spend the day getting splashed and possibly being thrown onto rocks or into churning water. We get to wear helmets."
"Awesome, what kind of helmets?"
"Not sure, I think they're probably like bicycle helmets."
"Sign me up then, that's my favourite type of helmet. How much will it cost?"
"$180 but that includes sex with the instructor afterwards."
"Woo."

I know a guy named Roger who got his bottom lip pierced because my friend Bill told him he looked like the lead singer from Blink 182. When he showed us afterwards, Bill said,

"Oh, I meant the lead singer from Phish." Roger's lip became infected and, despite a course of antibiotics, turned into what looked like mango puree. Eventually he had to have a chunk removed and the two sections of bottom lip sewn together. The reduced width pulled the top lips in at the sides and now he permanently looks like he is about to say something.

"And, if you look at the next slide, you'll see we have... yes Roger?"
"What? I didn't say anything."
"Sorry, I thought you were about t... yes Roger?"

When I was ten, my best friend Michael and I built a raft by duct-taping foam pool noodles to an old wooden pallet. Assuming the river down the road from my house eventually led to the ocean, we planned to ride the raft to the beach, make a day of it, then catch a bus home. Upon discovering the raft was only buoyant enough for one person, Michael waited onboard while I went home to get more pool noodles. When I got back, I discovered he had gone on without me so I went home.

Around 7pm that evening, Michael's mother rang my house asking as to his whereabouts. Around 9pm, the police had me show them where he had embarked from. He was located a few hours after that. Apparently, while waiting for me to return, Michael tried testing the raft by crossing the creek gondola-style with a long stick. Reaching the middle, he

found the stick wasn't long enough to reach the bottom and the raft drifted downstream in the current. After about fifteen miles, the river opened out into marshy flatlands. Finding himself bogged in reeds, Michael decided to evacuate the raft and wade back. When they discovered him, he was stuck in mud up to his chest, approximately ten feet from the raft. The next day's newspaper had a photo of him being pulled out with a strap, titled, "Boy builds raft, found after search." I was a bit annoyed at this as he didn't build the raft by himself and it had been my idea in the first place. We weren't allowed to hang around with each other after that.

Years later, my mother told me that Michael died while jumping off a roof into a pool and missing. Which was a bit sad. Some time after that I saw Michael collecting trollies at K-Mart. When I told my mother this, she said, "Oh I just told you that so you wouldn't do it."

My mother had also told me that my cousin Jeremy died from electrocution while reaching behind a refrigerator so I asked if I was likely to bump into him sometime as well.
"No," she answered, "I didn't lie about Jeremy dying. It wasn't by electrocution though, he was molested and killed by a pedophile."
"Oh my god, that's much worse," I said, "why didn't you just tell me that instead?"
"You kept fucking around behind the fridge."
"What about Uncle Carl?"

"No, he really did get hit by a train."

Uncle Carl really enjoyed tickling so the truth about Jeremy might have served as a much better warning. I stayed overnight at my uncle's house once while my parents were at the hospital with my sister. He convinced me to have a bath with him by telling me that it was a Japanese custom. He wasn't Japanese so I have no idea why I agreed to it, but we had been drinking saké beforehand which might have had something to with it. I was eight. Nobody got hurt though and we both got something out of it. Carl got to see me naked and I got a scarf when we went shopping the next day.

"It looks fantastic on you. Very Bohemian. You should try on these slacks as well."

My parents were sitting vigil at the hospital because my older sister Leith had swallowed twelve dollars in five-cent pieces and was being kept overnight for observation. It was the third time she had been admitted for swallowing coins. Nobody knew why she kept doing it. I asked Leith about it years later, and she said that she just liked the taste. Apparently she sucked the coins until they had no flavour left and then swallowed them so they didn't get mixed up with the unsucked coins.

Relatives probably told their children that Leith died doing it. We didn't leave the house much and rarely had visitors. As I wasn't allowed to play with Michael anymore, I mostly messed about with two brothers that lived in the house across the street. Scott and Craig Holland were older than me but they owned a go-cart and I owned an Atari. Their mother was divorced but she had a boyfriend named James Beauregard-Smith who spent a fair amount of time there.

Once, while I was at their house watching television, I spilled Coke on the couch. James grabbed me by the hair, called me a 'little cunt' and told me to go home. I heard shouting from the house behind me as I crossed the street. Later that evening, James strangled the mother after she told him she was going back to her ex-husband. He then chased Scott into the bathroom where Craig was having a bath, and drowned them both. Scott and his mother were found under a pile of leaves, Craig was found wrapped in a sheet under the floorboards.

I only learnt of these details many years later. At the time, when I enquired as to why Scott and Craig weren't around anymore, my mother told me that they had both gone out without jackets and died of hypothermia.

"Have they replaced me yet?" asked Simon, moving a pile of pizza boxes off a seat so I could sit down.
"We're doing a second round of interviews this week," I told him, "Not for a senior designer though, we're interviewing juniors. I'm fairly sure if you apologised to Mike though he would understand and..."
"I'm not apologising to anyone," Simon interrupted, "I'd

rather be stabbed than ever have to design another business card or logo again."

I could understand this. When I was in my teens, all I wanted to be was a graphic designer. I lived and breathed typography and identity, idolized the likes of Neville Brody and Designers Republic, and devoted four years to gaining my bachelor of visual communication. The excitement of a .x update to Freehand, Photoshop or MacOS would almost give me an aneurysm and if anyone mentioned they "need something for something", I was the first to raise my hand. Money didn't come into it. I once designed an eight page brochure in exchange for dog grooming clippers and thought it was a pretty good deal. I didn't even own a dog at the time. Twenty years later, I won't even design a missing cat poster without carrying on.

"What are you going to do instead?" I asked.
"I don't know yet," said Simon thoughtfully, "I might turn bowls."
"Bowls?"
"Wooden bowls. When my grandfather died, I got his wood-turning lathe. There's a market for wooden bowls."
"I'm sure there is. Do you know how to use a lathe?" I asked doubtfully.
"No, but how hard can it be? You throw on a big piece of wood, press the button, and cut off all the bits that don't look like a bowl. People like bowls. Especially those really wide shallow ones you put on a table. For fruit. Or keys and

lighters and sunglasses."

"Where are you going to sell them? Are you going to set up a booth at county fairs?"

"Maybe," said Simon, "I only just thought of the idea so I don't have all the details."

When I was in my first year of high school, a boy named George lost an eye because of a lathe. To 'turn' a piece of wood, you use something called a chuck-key - essentially a metal ratchet with handles - to tighten the jaws of a chuck which holds the wood securely. You then *ensure the chuck-key is removed* and press a big yellow button. This spins the chuck, along with whatever is held in its jaws, at horrendous speeds.

While demonstrating how to operate the lathe to a group of boys, including myself and George, who were told to gather around close and watch, our teacher Mr Williams forgot to remove the chuck key.

Afterwards, a few kids swore they had seen a blur as the chuck key left the chuck but I was watching pretty closely and didn't see anything. George's head was thrown back as if he had been kicked by a horse. His feet actually left the ground. As we all stared, in horrified shock, George climbed to his feet with a confused look on his face and put his hand up to his eye. Only the chuck-key's handle was visible. Surprisingly, there wasn't a lot of blood. Everybody yelled at the same time. Completely unaware of what was happening due to the noise of the lathe, Mr Williams continued his demonstration.

"Keep the chisel edge at a low angle... "
"MR WILLIAMS!"
"...otherwise it might grab. We don't want any accidents. As you can see, by applying pressure to only the areas you want removed, the candlestick begins to take shape."

Mr Williams was placed on leave after that and didn't come back. George returned after a month or so, but left again after his parents received a large settlement and enrolled him in a private school. He actually went on to take up archery and competed in the 2001 Special Olympics World Games, placing second for a silver medal. The person who took home gold only had missing legs which seems a bit unfair. They should probably have given George a chair and made the guy in a wheelchair wear a patch.

I lost sight in my left eye once. It was only for a few minutes after accidently stabbing myself with a drinking straw while driving but I know what it's like to live with a disability.

"Do you want to see a photo of him?" Simon asked.
"Who?"
"The guy she slept with," Simon said, grabbing his laptop, "he looks like an absolute dickhead."
He typed furiously then scrolled through the white-water rafting company's Facebook page.

"That's him, second on the right. His name is Douglas. Who the fuck is named Douglas? Look at what he's wearing."

Douglas wore white boardshorts with a blue palm-tree pattern, gold mirror sunglasses like the ones bicyclists wear, and a t-shirt that had 'F.B.I.' written in large letters with 'Female Body Inspector' smaller below. He had his tongue out and was making the 'gnarly' sign with a thumb and little finger.

"He's with the FBI," I said, "Maybe he only slept with Cathy as part of a sting operation."
"What? No, it's one of those piss-weak joke t-shirts that douchebags like Douglas think is hilarious."
"Women do like men in uniform though. And sailors. Perhaps it was the combination that drew Cathy to him in the first place."
"It's not a uniform and he's not a sailor," Simon spat, "He rides blow-up boats down a river for a living."
"Which makes him a sailor. People who spend their lives in boats are either fishermen or sailors and he's not wearing a beanie."
Simon slammed shut his laptop.
"If I go for a paddle in a canoe, it doesn't make me a sailor, it makes me a canoeist. He's more of a rafter."
"Like Tom Sawyer?"
"No, that was Huckleberry Finn. Tom Sawyer was the one who convinced other kids to paint a fence for him. And no, the raft that Huckleberry and Jim lived on was a proper raft.

White-water rafters don't even use a raft, they use a blow-up boat. They should have to call it white-water blow-up boating."

"Who's Jim?" I asked.

"He's the runaway slave that rafts down the river with Huckleberry."

"I thought his name was Uncle Tom."

"No, Uncle Tom makes rice. The kind you can microwave in the packet."

I've never been a big fan of 'the Classics'. I once had to read Alcott's *Little Women* for a school assignment and I figure that's enough of the Classics to keep me going for a while. It mainly consisted of girls talking about their feelings and complaining about things. There was also a guy who rode a horse.

"She told me that it was an accident," Simon said, "that she didn't mean for it to happen."

"No doubt," I agreed, "those inflatable boats are pretty bouncy. They probably went over a big bump in the river and she bounced onto his penis. I'm sure it happens all the time. They probably have you sign a waiver or something."

"No, that it was a mistake. Everyone got drunk afterwards."

"Ah, that explains it. It was probably slim pickings that day on the river but after several shots, Douglas thought, 'What the hell, I'll do her from behind so I don't have to look at her face.'"

I'd met Cathy a few times, mainly at work functions, and Simon had a photo of both of them on his desk for years. The photo showed Simon, wearing a dark grey suit with light blue shirt and leather business slippers, with his arm around a short chubby girl wearing an ankle length purple velvet dress. The dress had long sleeves that flared at the ends and a wide neck opening. Around her neck, she wore a black choker with a star pendant in the centre. Her dark hair, parted in the middle, hung straight down. She looked like a gothic Teletubbie.

"Is your girlfriend a Goth?" I'd asked Simon the first time I saw the photo.

"No dickhead, she's a wicken."

"A what?"

"She practices Wicca. It's a modern religion based on pagan rituals."

"Right, so she's an unemployed Art's graduate then."

"No, she works in a call centre."

"Did you stop for a photo opportunity on the way to a forest-clearing candle dance?"

"No, it was my Grandpa's funeral."

Apparently Cathy had written and read a poem for the service. Simon showed me the folded A4 program they gave out to those attending. Below a photo of an old man holding a shovel, the poem read;

Cry not.
I reach to the universe and she embraces me.
I welcome her arms. We merge.
I feel everything. Everything that has ever been and will ever be.
I feel her strength. I feel her love. I feel the universe.
I cannot see your tears though.
Cry not.

"Wow," I told him, "that's pretty fucking dreadful. And I think the word Universe is meant to be capitalised. Also, your grandpa doesn't look like he was the kind of person to care about hugs from the Universe. She should probably have written a poem about shovels."

Simon nodded, "Or woodwork. He had a big shed. He also collected World War 2 memorabilia."

"Anything good?"

"Mostly just Nazi stuff. Uniforms and knives. That kind of thing."

When I die, I do not want anyone reading any poems at my service. Certainly not terrible ones. And there had better not be any singing either. I'd actually prefer not to have a service. If it was legal, I'd just have my body dropped off at a vet's office. A cardboard box containing my ashes could be picked up a few weeks later and scattered somewhere nice. Or out of the window on the drive home, I don't care. I have told my partner Holly this which means there will probably be singing and poems and the worst photo she can find of me enlarged and stuck in an A-frame. Probably the one where I am about to take a bite out of a hotdog.

Simon looked horrified. "What's that meant to mean?"

"I'm just saying. Ignoring the fact that Douglas dresses and acts like an idiot, he's fairly fit, tanned and muscular - paddling all day will do that to you - whereas Cathy is more... circular. And gothic."

"Wicken," Simon corrected.

"Whatever. They're all dreadful. And since when do Wickens go white-water rafting? It's just weird. If I was spending a day by the river, the last thing I would want to see is a boat bobbing past me with the chick from *The Ring* sitting in it."

"Her sister wanted to do it," explained Simon, "what's your point?"

"My point is, generalising of course, that most people who go white-water rafting are the healthy, attractive, outdoors type. Like Douglas. I can see how Cathy - hundreds of miles away from home and charged with adrenaline after an exciting shared experience - might be susceptible to his advances, but obviously the choices were limited that day for Douglas. He probably had to stay back late to deflate the rafts or something and by the time he got to the bar, his coworkers had already claimed the good looking ones."

"How can you say that? She's beautiful."

"She's beautiful to you because you love her. Or think you do. I've always thought she was a bit of a bushpig."

When someone breaks up with his partner, for whatever reason, it is probably best to simply say, "I understand you being upset, she/he had many defining qualities," and perhaps follow this up by nodding. Nobody will ask, "like what?" even if they want to, so after they nod along for a bit, you can go back to doing whatever it is you'd rather be doing than talking about feelings. If people were meant to talk about feelings, they'd be called talkings. You're not meant to say anything bad about the person they have broken up with because when they inevitably get back together, it will be held against you.

"How's it going with you and your girlfriend Louise?"
'We went through a rough patch and broke up..."
"Well you dodged a bullet. Louise is a fat girl's name and horrible to say. Its almost as bad as the name Gwyneth. Both names sound like they are being squeezed out of a balloon. Plus, I heard Louise sucked off a dog once."
"Then we worked through our issues and got back together. She's just gone to the ladies and will be back in a minute."

I went to school with a girl named Louise. She was a huge heifer with tight curly hair and a moustache. Once during a school game of soccer, she ran to the edge of the playing field, dropped her shorts, and did a poo. This is the kind of thing people named Louise do. The gym teacher had to pick it up with a plastic shopping bag.

I also knew a Gwyneth once. She was bi-polar and stabbed

her boyfriend Stuart in the arm with a steak-knife during an argument about electric cars. It was the second worst dinner party I have ever been to. The worst dinner party I have ever been to was when Gwyneth and Stuart held another one six months later and I was the only person who turned up. I made a joke about swapping the cutlery with plastic utensils and Gwyneth cried.

"A bushpig?" Simon asked incredulously, "because she didn't shave her armpits?"
"No, she just looked like a bushpig. She didn't shave her armpits?"
"What the fuck is a bushpig?"
"I don't know. A pig that lives in a bush I guess."
Simon opened his laptop again and typed 'bushpig' into Google.
"According to Wikipedia, it's a member of the pig family that lives in forests, woodland, riverine vegetation and reed beds in East and Southern Africa. It looks like a big hairy rat."

I'm a big fan of Wikipedia. If my partner Holly and I are having a fight about something and I know I'm wrong, I change the facts on the Wikipedia page to side with my error and then tell her to look it up;

"Well I'll be, Tom Sellek of *Magnum P.I.* fame *was* in the band Hall & Oats. I apologise for doubting you. I just figured the band's name was made up of their last names."

If I'd known Simon was going to look up bushpig, I would have changed the existing Wikipedia photo to one of Cathy beforehand because it would have been hilarious.

"That works," I said, "I wouldn't usually say such a thing, but she really was dreadful. I've always thought you could do a lot better."

"Really?" asked Simon.

"Of course. You have many defining qualities."

"Like what?" It's allowed if you're asking about yourself and you say it in a kind of sarcastic self-deprecating manner.

"Oh I don't know, you own your own apartment. Not many people can say that. Plus it looks a lot better now without all the candles and dreamcatchers everywhere. The macramé wall hanging you had above the fireplace didn't really go with all your mid-century modern furniture."

Simon rubbed the arm of his chair, "It's Herman Miller."

"Yes I know. Very nice. Did she actually own any furniture? I don't see anything missing."

"No," Simon replied, "Not much. She always said possessions end up owning you."

"That's just something poor people say to make it look like they have any choice. You know what would look good on the wall above the fireplace? A large framed Rothko print."

Simon nodded. "What else?"

"Maybe a new rug. There's candle wax on this one. You might be able to get it out with an iron and brown paper though."

"No, I meant what else apart from owning my own apartment."

"Well... you also own a lathe. And you're a snappy dresser. Not right at this moment obviously, but you scrub up alright."

"I do own a lot of Diesel and G-Star..."

"And your head isn't nearly as big as I make it out to be. You kind of look like Dave Matthews."

"The musician? I like him."

"Of course you do. He has many defining qualities."

Simon nodded. "We have the same haircut."

"That's true. Any woman would be lucky to have you."

I glanced around the apartment. "Do you want me to help you clean up in here a bit?"

"Okay."

Tudor

I was once asked, "I liked that Australian man who got stabbed by a swordfish. Did you know him?"

I never met Steve Irwin but I did once go fishing with Greg Norman and Matt Lattanzi. Greg Norman is famous for accurately hitting balls with sticks and Matt Lattanzi isn't famous for anything apart from once being married to Olivia Newton John. My friend Bill, who ran an Australian tourism publication, invited me out for the day.

"What do you do?" asked Matt Lattanzi.
"I work for a design agency," I told him.
"Ah, so you're good at drawing pictures and shit?"
"Something like that. What do *you* do?"
"He's an actor," Greg Norman answered, "Did you ever see the movie *Xanadu*? He's in it. He dances on rollerskates."

I was quite young when the movie *Xanadu* came out in theatres but not too young to be impressed by Olivia Newton John's outfit. I remember being puzzled as to why *all* girls didn't choose to wear flowing white dresses, ribbons in their hair, and roller skates. I wasn't so impressed with Olivia's outfit in *Grease* although the shiny black pants she wore at the end were ok.

My best friend at the time owned a copy of the album *Physical* which came with a folded poster showing Olivia doing exercises in Spandex leggings and leg warmers. Where the crotch was meant to be, he had made a hole.

"Why is there a hole in the poster?"
"It came that way."
"But it's all wet."
"Just fold it up and put it back in the cover."

"I've been in more than that," Matt Lattanzi said defensively, "Did you ever see the television series *Paradise Beach*?"
"No."
"Well I was in it. I played Cooper Hart. What about the movie *My Tutor*?"
"No. Is it about someone who owns an English cottage?"
"What?"
"Did you say tudor or tutor?"
"Tutor. What the fuck is tudor?"
"It's an architectural style popularised in England during the 1500's."
"Why the fuck would anybody make a movie about that? It's about a guy who has an affair with his French tutor."
He pointed a thumb at me and turned to Greg Norman, "Get a load of this guy, fucking asking me if I was in a movie about old English cottages. Who invited him?"

I also had a cup of magic tea with Kate Bush once.

After my parents divorced in the eighties, my mother became a social worker, and a lesbian, and began hanging around with 'artistic types'. Before the divorce, my parent's friends mainly consisted of people they knew from their local tennis club. They were all very polite and well dressed and sometimes we had parties at our place where everyone would stand around eating fondue while Boney-M albums played in the background at a level that wouldn't hinder conversation.

"Fantastic fondue guys, what kind of cheese do you use?"
"Kraft."
"Delicious. I also love this album. Boney M are going to be the next Beatles. You mark my words. Have you heard the track, Ra Ra Rasputin?"
"Yes, fantastic isn't it? It's just called Rasputin though."
"Is it?"
"Yes. They sing Ra Ra Rasputin in the song but it's just called Rasputin."
"Well there you go. I did not know that."

My father moved out while my mother was at the local pool with my sister and I. The swimming centre was having the grand opening of their newly installed waterslide that day and had advertised heavily. We stood in line for about thirty minutes but before we even got to the steps, a foundation gave way and the lower half of the slide separated, moving several feet to the right. There were two kids who had just pushed off from the top, a chubby girl in her early teens and her younger brother who sat between her legs. Their exit opened to a thirty foot plunge onto concrete. I like to think that the chubby girl purposely landed below her bother. He survived.

They closed the swimming centre and we returned home to discover my father's clothes, the Bang & Olufsen stereo system, and all the Boney M albums missing. According to the letter he left on the dining table, he loved my mother and his children, but he was *in* love with the lady that did the member's fees and match scheduling at their tennis club.

My mother didn't play tennis after that, she instead devoted most of her time to crying, yelling, and telling me terrible stories about my father.

"Your father is a sick pervert, sometimes when we made love, he liked to stick his finger in my bottom."

I was eleven. I spent a lot of time in my room. I read a lot. I was tall for my age and when I walked down the hallway across wooden floorboards, my mother would rush out of her bedroom screaming that it sounded like how my father walks and for me to take smaller steps. I learnt to walk like the guy in *Dune* does to avoid the giant sandworm eating him and only when I had to. There was no point walking down the hallway several times a day when I could cut this down to just a few by storing food in my closet and urinating out the window.

Late one evening, I opened my window, pulled out my penis, and began urinating into the backyard. It was dark but there was a full moon. As I was standing there, staring into the night, something caught my eye peripherally to the left. I squinted and realised it was a man standing very still against the wall. He realised I had seen him and leapt at me. I threw myself back, narrowly avoiding his reach as he tried to grab me through the window. We stared at each other for a few moments then he smiled and disappeared into the darkness. I couldn't close my window for fear of him jumping out and grabbing me and as far as I knew, he was still in the backyard. *Or, in the house,* I thought, *perhaps he was walking silently down the hallway towards...* My bedroom door opened. I yelled.

"What are you doing?" My mother asked, "Why is your penis out? Were you masturbating?"
"A man tried to grab me," I pointed at the window as I pulled up and zipped my pants.
'What?"
"A man. He was standing outside and he tried to grab me. He's in the backyard."
"There's piss all over the floor you filthy animal. Clean that up and stop telling lies. You're just like your father."

She slapped me hard on the side of the head a few times and slammed the door on her way out. I sat on my bed staring at the open window for the rest of the night. I almost nodded off a few times but the instant I closed my eyes, the image of the man smiling at me through the window bolted me back awake. The moment the sun came up, I closed and locked the window, pulled the curtains across, and never opened them again.

I have no idea who the man was or what he was doing outside my window, but I saw him a few years later and recognised him instantly. He was at Target, a few people ahead of me in line at the checkout, buying lambswool car seat covers.

After several months of tears, terrible stories and stride critique, my mother decided to study towards a sociology degree and enrolled as a full time student. When she wasn't at university, she locked herself in her bedroom to study or went out with her uni friends. My sister Leith and I were kind of left to our own devices during that time. Leith went out a lot. She had a boyfriend named Trevor who had long curly hair and owned a metallic blue panel van with the members of the band KISS painted on the side. Trevor also had one leg shorter than the other and had a special shoe with a three inch heel. He enjoyed giving me dead arms so one day I did a poo in a plastic bag and wiped it into the air vents of his car. He died in a car crash. Not because of the poo, apparently he was low on fuel so switched the car off to coast down a big hill. At the bottom, he tried to turn and the steering lock engaged. He went through the front window of a H&R Block and was decapitated by a giant green square. I caught the bus with my sister to his funeral.

They played *Love Gun*.

Back then, milk was delivered during the night so if you wanted two bottles of milk in the morning, you left two empty bottles on your doorstep with the money under them. Sneaking up driveways in the middle of the night and taking the money was known as 'doing the milk rounds' and would generally net you a few dollars. My bike was stolen one night and for several months I did the milk rounds so I could afford to catch the bus to school. I was chased by the occupants a few times but had a large stride for my age. I didn't tell my mother my bike had been stolen and she never noticed.

I moved out of home about the same time my mother graduated. I was fourteen. At that age, I spent a lot of my free time hanging out with school friends at a local shopping mall called Tea Tree Plaza. We generally just sat on benches and smoked cigarettes to look cool while pointing out how lame everyone else was.

This was years before anyone had an issue with cigarettes or cigarette advertising. Both my parents had smoked. They smoked Winfield's because that was the brand Paul Hogan smoked and advertised. They smoked in the house, they smoked while playing tennis, and they smoked in the car. Sometimes when we were on family trips, I could barely see out the windows.

"Why are you coughing? You'd better not be getting sick."
"It's smoky in here. Can I wind down my window?"
"No, the air conditioner is on. I don't know what you're carrying on about, your mother and I are the ones smoking and we're not coughing."
"Just a little bit? I can't breathe."
"Fine. Just half an inch though. You can stick your drinking straw through the gap and breath through that if you are going to be a dickhead about it."
"How long before we get there?"
"Six or seven hours. It depends on the traffic."

Outside tobacconist stores, representatives from different tobacco companies would stand with trays of samples asking things like, "Would you like to try our new smoother tasting menthol?" in order to persuade people to change over to their particular brand. One called me over.

"How old are you?" asked the middle-aged lady wearing a gold Benson & Hedges jacket.
"Sixteen," I lied.
"Would you like to make twenty dollars?"

All I had to do was wear her jacket and offer people cigarettes while she went shopping, "for an hour or so." I agreed. Immediately after she left, kids from school came over and grabbed handfuls of cigarettes. I thought I might get in trouble for this but when the lady - whose name was Rachael - eventually returned three hours later, she was delighted at how many cigarettes were gone.

"What are you doing tomorrow?" she asked.
Tomorrow was a school day.
"Nothing," I told her.

Within a week, I was working everyday from 9am to 3pm with an hour break for lunch. I was given my own gold jacket, a pair of black trousers, leather shoes and a white shirt. The pay was sixty dollars per day, in cash, which was more money than I had ever had in my life. I'd seen a movie in which a book had the pages hollowed out to make a hiding spot so I made one out of a dictionary and hid my growing collection of twenty dollar bills. The school rang to check where I was after a while but my sister pretended she was our mother and told them I had broken my leg and would be in hospital for a few months. I bought her a pair of Ugg boots. I bought myself a replacement bike. Then a car.

I hadn't intended on buying a car, but a guy who worked at the shoe store across from the tobacconist told me he was selling his 1973 Honda Civic hatchback for $400 which seemed like a bargain. It was bright yellow and had mag wheels and a working cassette player. He included a steering wheel lock and a cassingle of *Hold Me Now* by The Thompson Twins.

As I couldn't let my mother find out about the vehicle, I parked it a few streets from our house. Each morning, when

I was meant to be heading to school, I would ride my bike to the car, put the bike in the back, change into my uniform, and drive to work.

Being fourteen, I didn't have a driver's licence, but the route to Tea Tree Plaza involved crossing several intersections and roundabouts so I learnt the road rules fairly quickly. Occasionally, I would break out in a sweat when police cars were behind me at traffic lights, especially as the Honda stalled a lot, but I always stayed under the speed limit and used my indicators so I was lucky enough never to be pulled over. I stayed on side streets wherever possible.

The school eventually rang again but Leith told them that I had cancer and wouldn't be back until my radiation therapy sessions were completed. I bought her a Yamaha organ. She made it look dirty by rubbing Nutella over the keys so our mother would believe a friend lent it to her.

"Where'd that come from?"
"Sarah lent it to me. You don't know her. She got a new keyboard for her birthday so she said I could borrow this dirty old one."
"Why does the cat keep licking it?"

After three months, Rachael asked me if I wanted to make extra money doing 'club promotions' on Friday and Saturday nights. I told my mother that I had applied for a night job stacking shelves for a local supermarket. No, it wouldn't interfere with my school work and yes, I would be careful riding home after dark.

It was essentially the same thing I had been doing - giving people cigarettes - but in nightclubs and for a different brand called Horizon. I had to be at the company's office at 9pm where I changed into an outfit consisting of white shoes, white pants, white shirt with Horizon branding, and a guest-pass badge. The back of my car was loaded with boxes of cigarettes and promotional items and I was given a list, with the names and addresses of ten popular nightclubs to visit, and a street directory. I drove to the first club, where I was waved in by bouncers, and gave out cigarettes and branded lighters from a big bag to patrons until I ran out. Then I drove to the next club, filled the bag from the rear of my hatchback, and repeated the process.

Before doing club promotions, I hadn't known such places even existed. I had been to a few school discos but these didn't prepare me for the real experience. There were strobes and smoke machines and really good music with bass - lots of bass - from really big speakers and people danced with each other without being made to by teachers. Not all of the clubs on the list were as exciting as others, piano bars for instance, but these were still interesting and there was only a couple of those as younger smokers were the target demographic.

"How did you do last night?" Rachael asked me.

"Good," I replied.

"How many on the list did you get through?"

"All of them."

'All of them? How much product did you give away?'

"All of it. Lerox, The Toucan and The Mars Bar were the best, I could have done triple the amounts there. You should give me more for those clubs tonight."

Within a few months, I was the promotion company's model employee. Because I loved doing it. As I was 'in uniform' with a guest-pass, nobody ever asked my age or to see ID and I gave whole packs to the people working at the entrances so after the first few weeks they knew me by name. I made friends. The DJ at Lerox gave me a set of Senheiser earphones and played tracks I requested. A girl who worked behind the bar at The Toucan gave me my first kiss. She had purple hair. A transsexual who worked at The Mars Bar told me she loved me and made me a Duran Duran mix tape.

The Mars Bar was the only gay club on my list. I'd had no prior experience with gay people apart from schoolyard discussions and my father's warnings about 'poofters'. Whenever my father said the word 'poofter', he would bend his hand downwards to indicate a limp wrist. There was a boy at school with partial paralysis in his right arm that caused his hand to do the same thing so for years I thought my father was refering to people with this condition.

"Look at that guy in the wheelchair. He's all bent up and

shaking."

"Yes, he must have advanced poofter."

I'd been to The Mars Bar about twenty times and nobody had tried to 'bum' me. It was just another club. It had good music, a good atmosphere, and everyone seemed to be having fun. The only difference was that boys kissed boys, boys kissed boys dressed like girls, and girls kissed girls. Girls didn't kiss boys dressed like girls. Occasionally guys, usually older men, would flirt and carry on a bit but it was generally good natured. I'd tell them I was straight and they'd tell me I was in denial and offer me drinks that I wouldn't accept because I was working. Not once did I drink alcohol and not once did I feel in danger. I was friends with the bouncers and they were always nearby.

At around 2am on a Friday night at The Mars Bar, I approached a booth of about eight people. The booth was in a dark corner furthest away from the strobe lighting and dancing.

"Hi, I see you're smokers," I said, noting the packs of cigarettes and ashtrays on their table, "Would you care to try a Horizon?"
"David?"

My mother and I stared at each other for a moment before she leapt out of her seat and started laying into me. She slapped and screamed. With military precision, the bouncers were on her within seconds. One gabbed her hair and yanked her sideways onto the floor. Another grabbed her ankles and dragged her out. It was over in under ten seconds but the look on her face, before her shirt caught on the carpet and pulled over her head, was the last image I had of my mother for many years.

I slept in my car that night. The next morning I parked down the street from our house and watched. After a few hours, a police car pulled up and two officers went inside. They left twenty minutes later and my mother pulled out of the driveway a few minutes after that. I drove to the house, let myself in, and took the hollowed out dictionary containing my money.

While doing cigarette promotions, I had met the owner of a popular bar and hotel called The Austral. Her name was Carol and she was in her late fifties. Her husband had died in a motorcycle accident a few years earlier and she managed the establishment herself with five or six staff members. We got along well so I drove to The Austral and asked her how much the rooms were per night.

"Alright, talk to me, what's going on?" she asked.
I blurted out everything.
"I'm only fourteen and I've been doing cigarette promotions and I bought a car and my mum got dragged out of The Mars Bar by her ankles and now I don't have anywhere to live."

I might have also cried a bit.

I stayed at The Austral for over a year. I didn't have to pay for my room or meals but I did help in the kitchen and in the bar emptying ashtrays, washing glasses and writing questions for quiz nights. I was also given a few dollars here and there. I missed my fifteenth birthday. I only realised a few weeks after. There was a roof outside my window and often, I would climb out onto it and read. A few doors down from The Austral, there was a second hand bookstore called Second Print owned by an old man named Bernard. I spent a lot of time there, it had an entire wall devoted to science fiction and most of the books were priced between ten and thirty cents. The store didn't get many customers and Bernard read most of the day so he was happy for me to do the same in a corner. One day he closed his book and asked me if I knew how to play chess. I didn't so he collected a chess board and pieces from the back room and taught me. We played most days after that. I also helped out in the store. Once, when I was helping Bernard put books he had just bought on shelves, I noticed he had numbers tattooed on his left forearm. I asked him about them but he rolled his sleeves down and changed the subject. He lent me books. He liked the author John Wyndham.

"Read this one. *The Crysalids*. It's about repression of knowledge and fear of change. You'll like it. It's got kids your age in it."
"It sounds dreadful."

"Just fucking read it. And watch the store for ten minutes. I need to take a dump."

On my sixteenth birthday, Carol knocked on the door of my room. She told me a police officer was downstairs and wanted to speak to me in regards to an ongoing missing person report. I collected what I could carry and left out the window.

I slept in the back room of Second Print for a few months. Bernard gave me an inflateable camping mattress and sleeping bag to use. He also gave me a part time job. I wasn't paid a set wage, he just asked me at the end of each day how much I needed. One day Bernard stopped coming in to work. I opened and closed the store for a couple of days until Bernard's sister came in and told me that Bernard had died and the shop was closing. Later, it became an adult clothing store called Puss in Boots.

I took what money was in the till, the chess set, and several hardcover first edition John Wyndham novels. I slept in my car for the next few weeks. During the day, I would go to a park to read or walk around the city. I ate a lot at McDonald's. Often, I would go to a music store called Andromeda Records and listen to albums. They had a comfortable couch with a pair of earphones and even though I never bought anything, the owner, a large bearded man named Maurice, didn't care how long I stayed. Maurice didn't like people, especially people who took records out of sleeves or asked about Compact Discs, but we got on alright. He was really into model building and after closing one night, I helped him assemble and paint a plastic ED209 robot. I wasn't actually allowed to assemble or paint anything but I handed him things when he asked and we chatted about our favourite science fiction authors. He gave me a copy of *Ender's Game* to read. The next day, when Maurice was busy yelling at a customer and the phone rang, he asked me to answer it. I just kind of worked there after that. There was no discussion about it, he simply passed me a Motörhead t-shirt and said, "Here put this on. If you're going to work here then at least look the fucking part."

It was while working at Andromeda Records, I bumped into the DJ I knew from Lerox. His name was Simon Lewicki. We chatted and he told me that he and his girlfriend were looking for a flatmate. I moved into their rented two bedroom apartment that night. I didn't have any furniture in my room but there was a couch on the back deck that Simon and I carried to my room for me to use. I woke up the first night covered in baby spiders, there was a nest under the springs of the couch the size of a watermelon. I bought a bed. And a bookshelf.

At night, when Simon wasn't working clubs, we listened to music and he showed me how to sample sounds on his Atari ST. We also spent a lot of time discussing good DJ names.

"It has to be something that says 'I absolutely kill the beat.'"

"What about Groove Terminator?"

"No, that's stupid. It's not 1970. Who says the word groove?"

After six months, we received an eviction notice due to multiple noise complaints from neighbours. Around the same time, my boss Maurice was arrested for tax evasion and Andromeda Records was placed into liquidation. I turned up to work one morning to discover chains and padlocks on the doors. I knew the lock on the bathroom window was faulty so I climbed in and took Maurice's ED209, a couple of t-shirts, and a life-sized cardboard cut-out of Kim Wilde.

A friend of Simon's helped us move out of the apartment using a horse trailer. He told me that his parents, who owned a horse riding school, were looking for a stablehand. The position included room and board so I took it. Simon was a little annoyed at this, as we had originally planned to move together, but he and his girlfriend fought a lot - mainly about him getting a 'real job' - so I'd wanted to leave months before. Years later, Simon went on to have quite a bit of commercial success, releasing several singles and two top-selling albums in Australia. His girlfriend was probably all nice and encouraging then.

While I was working at the riding school, I saw a dog named Pete get kicked in the head by a horse. It killed him instantly. The owner, a man named John who had very wrinkly skin and bad teeth, rushed to Pete, placed his entire mouth over the dog's face, and gave mouth to mouth resuscitation. Pete revived and seemed fine but he could never turn left after that. If you were to his left and called, he had to do a right hand 270° turn. A few weeks later, I also got kicked in the head. It felt like a sledgehammer and I was lifted off my feet. I was dazed and bleeding but jumped up quickly to avoid John thinking I required assistance.

John and his wife Rose had an Amiga 500 on an old desk in their living room next to a maple and glass cabinet full of ceramic horse figurines. They didn't mind me using it so, after hours, I taught myself how to use a program called Deluxe Paint. Eventually I became responsible for designing advertisements and brochures for their business, which I liked doing a lot more than raking up manure and dodging kicks.

In those days, before email, I had to take the files to a printer on disk. After chatting with the manager of a printing firm called Finsbury Press several times, I was offered the position of junior in-house designer. The pay was four times what I was making at the riding school and I didn't have to get up at 5am so I agreed and rented a small apartment close by.

I quickly became good friends with one of my coworkers. His name was Geoffrey and he was really into dressing up as a knight and rushing at people with a sword in forests. Geoffrey was also really into Macs and convinced me to buy one. I learned Photoshop and Freehand, discovered

Fontographer, and collected typefaces as fanatically as Geoffrey collected *Magic: The Gathering* cards. I applied to university for a bachelor's degree in visual communication.

At the university interview, a design lecturer named Fred Littlejohn noted that I had included reading as a hobby on my application.

"Who's your favourite author?" he asked as another lecturer flicked through my portfolio of work making 'hmmm' noises.

"John Wyndam. He's a British science fiction writer."

"Really? And what's your favourite John Wyndham novel?"

"*The Crysalids*." I answered, "It's remarkable. I also like *Trouble With Lichen*."

Fred smiled. "*Consider Her Ways* is my favourite John Wyndham novel. Have you read it? It's certainly up there with *Trouble With Lichen*. You might also like the author Robert C. O'Brien."

Fred also liked Macs. I was accepted into the course.

During class, in the second year of my studies, the head of the school knocked on the classroom door and politely asked to speak with me. I accompanied him to his office where a female plain-clothes police officer was waiting. I wasn't arrested or anything, the officer just asked if I was doing ok, told me that I should consider contacting my mother sometime, and said that she was filing the missing person report as closed. I was twenty. I received a letter from my mother a few weeks later. It was addressed care of the University. It was three pages long and went on about how some parents lose sight of what matters and forget to be a parent and how she was proud of me. I didn't need her to be proud of me and I didn't contact her.

In my third year of uni, my sister phoned me at the semi-detached I was renting with two other students. Student registry gave her my number. I went with her to our grandfather's funeral a few days later and we sat next to our mother. My mother cried when she saw me. She looked old. We didn't hug and it felt weird to call her 'mum' so I just said, 'Hello Diane."

Afterwards, Diane invited my sister and I back to her house. We chatted, mainly small talk but broaching on the time between when we had last been in contact. It was awkward. I know I should have been interested in what she had been up to for the past several years but I wasn't. I didn't know her and I wished I hadn't gone to my grandfather's funeral. I didn't know him either. I feigned interest but I didn't care that Diane was now a social worker and most of her friends were also social workers. Or that she'd turned lesbian, then straight for a brief stint, then lesbian again and was currently 'close friends' with a local artist named Magenta Deluxe. Or that Magenta had taken her name from a paint swatch and was really into painting people's aura's.

As I was about to make my excuses to leave, Magenta arrived at the house. She was a large woman with bright red dyed hair and matching red shirt and pants. She looked like a giant chili pepper. She had two friends with her, a petite woman with long curly hair and a bald guy who was carrying a pottery teapot and small bowl. Diane and Magenta hugged.

"You must be David," Magenta stated. She threw out her arms and hugged me enthusiastically, "Diane has told me so much about you."

"Yes," I replied, "I'm sure she has. The stories probably had a few gaps in them though."

"A few. You have to let me paint your aura," she continued, "it's very interesting. Predominately green with red spikes."

"That sounds dreadful. Some other time perhaps, I was just about to leave."

"No, stay and chat with us for a bit. This is Terry, he's a social worker." I shook hands with the bald guy.

"And this is my dear friend Kate who is visiting from England."

I shook Kate Bush's hand.

See, I was getting to it. A thousand pages back you were probably asking yourself, "Who the fuck cares? What does any of this have to do with drinking a cup of magic tea with Kate Bush? And who the fuck is Kate Bush?"

"Nice to meet you.' I said, "Are you an artist or a social worker?"

Kate smiled, "An artist. What do *you* do?"

"He's in his third year at Uni," my mother answered, "he's

going to be a graphic designer."

"Oh lovely," Kate smiled, "I know a lot of graphic designers. You can't swing a cat in the Sulhamstead pub without hitting one."

"Where's Somersault?" I asked, not really caring.

"Sulhamstead. It's in Berkshire. I bought a tudor cottage there."

"Nice. What's tudor?"

"It's an architectural style popular in England during the 1500's."

"You couldn't afford something a bit newer?" I asked.

Kate laughed and turned to Diane, "He has to join the circle and share tea with us. "

The bald guy named Terry moved the coffee table to the side of the living room and positioned six cushions on the floor in a circle. He placed the pottery teapot and bowl in the middle. Everybody sat and Kate looked up at me, patting the cushion next to her.

"Actually, I appreciate the offer but I should head off..."

"Oh you must," Kate grabbed my hand and pulled me down, "It's magic tea."

"Well I'm certainly not drinking it then. What's magic about it?"

"It's an ancient Celtic recipe made with herbs," she explained, "and forest fungus."

"I'd probably prefer Lipton's."

Kate ignored me, "Okay, everybody hold hands."

"Really?" Diane was sitting to my right and that would mean holding her hand for the first time since I was a child.
'Yes, we have to close the circle."

Kate held my hand and I held Diane's. It was wrinkly and dry. I wished I had left. Everybody closed their eyes while Kate recited something about a goddess and balance. It was all fairly stupid. When she finally released my hand, I quickly released Diane's.

"We welcome David to the circle," Kate announced, "and share this gift with him."

She poured tea into the bowl and offered it to me ceremoniously. I took the bowl and raised it to my nose cautiously, the tepid liquid smelt like dishwater and had the same colour. Figuring it was better to get it over with quickly, I threw the contents back and swallowed quickly trying to avoid my tastebuds.

"Oh my god!" yelled the bald guy named Terry, "He drank it all!"
"I wasn't meant to?"
Kate stared at me in horror. "You were meant to share it with the circle. What the fuck?" She grabbed the bowl from my hands.
"Should we induce vomiting?" my mother asked.
Magenta jumped to her feet, "I'll see if there is any milk of magnesia in the medicine cabinet."

"No," the bald man named Terry said, "Milk of magnesia is for constipation and heartburn. You're supposed to give plain milk for poisoning."

Magenta searched the refrigerator, "Will soy milk work?"

I was panicking a bit at this point, "I drank poison? Why would you give me poison? Am I going to die?"

"What part of the word sharing don't you grasp?" Kate asked admonishingly, "You were meant take a small sip and pass it to the person on your left."

"Well you should have fucking told me that beforehand. I don't know the rules of the circle game. Why are you drinking poison? Is this a cult?"

"His aura is turning orange," shouted Magenta from the kitchen.

"Should we take him to the hospital?" Diane asked.

"No, he'll be fine," Magenta said, handing me a glass of milk. She was still in the kitchen but her arm stretched twenty feet into the living room like the rubber guy from *Fantastic Four* and snapped back when I took the glass.

"How did you do that? I asked.

"It's starting," said the bald guy named Terry.

Time snapped back a few seconds.

"It's starting," said the bald guy named Terry.

"I feel weird," I said, "Perhaps I *should* go to the hospital."

"You're going to be alright," Kate told me.

I blinked.

Everyone was sitting at the dining table eating pasta.

I blinked again.

I was standing outside watching them eat pasta through the

kitchen window. I held my eyes open to avoid blinking and heard a noise that sounded like a hundred people saying the word 'stick' at the same time.

"It's starting," said the bald guy named Terry.

"Right, I really *do* think I should go to the hospital." I said.

I blinked.

It was dark outside. Leith was gone. Diane, Kate and the bald guy named Terry were in the kitchen cooking pasta. Magenta was painting my aura while I sat on a stool in the living room. There was a mirror on the wall behind her and I could see the painting reflected. It looked like a squashed frog.

"Oh no," I said, "I knew it would be dreadful."

Blink.

The bald guy named Terry was playing an acoustic guitar. I was clapping to keep the beat. Diane and Magenta were curled up on the couch asleep at each end, Kate sat cross-legged in the middle making patterns on the wall with a laser pointer in time to the music. I couldn't stop clapping but I managed to turn to her and say, "I hate all of you."

I blinked. The blink was much longer this time.

I woke up just after 4am and gazed around. The lights were off and the only illumination came from the television screen. A documentary about Antarctica showed a sad looking bear floating on a piece of ice. I blinked hard a few times as a test but nothing changed. Diane and Magenta had gone to bed. Kate was asleep in a sitting position on the couch with her head lolled back snoring. My head was in her lap. The bald guy named Terry was on his knees giving me a blowjob.

I didn't visit Diane again.

My only other 'brush with fame' is having Simon LeBon's bodyguard ask me to move down two seats. I was waiting for a friend at the Hilton bar in Adelaide when Simon LeBon and a large man in a tight suit exited the elevator and headed over. This was well after the height of Duran Duran's fame and I think they were playing cabarets and cruise ships by then. The large man in a tight suit tapped me on the shoulder and asked, "Would you mind moving down two seats?" and I did. That's pretty much it for my part in the whole thing but I was close enough to hear their conversation. The bartender who served them asked, "Aren't you that guy from that band?"

Simon nodded, "Duran Duran."

"That's it. I liked that song you did about a hungry wolf. What was it called? I'm a Hungry Wolf or something?"

"Hungry *Like* the Wolf," Simon answered.

"That's the one. Very catchy. That other one was good too, what was it called, Tainted Love, did you do that as well?"

I wanted to yell, "No, that was Soft Cell. Duran Duran did Girls on Film, Planet Earth, Is There Something I should Know, My Own Way, The Chauffer and many other top ten hits," thinking Simon might be impressed by my knowledge and we would become best friends, but I didn't.

Simon nodded and said, "Yep."

Tasmania

"We should go to Tasmania," Geoffrey stated.

He turned his laptop towards me to present a photo of a woman posing on a trail in a rainforest. Geoffrey and I had been friends since working together at a printing firm years before. He was currently employed as a tech specialist for a local school and I was in my fourth and final year of studies. It was April, 1996.

"Why," I asked, "would I want to go to Tasmania?"
"Just to have a look," he replied, "It's supposed to be nice. It's the Apple Isle."

Tasmania is at the bottom of Australia, to the right, separated from the mainland by ocean. It's shaped kind of like an apple and its main export to the mainland is apples. It gets left off a lot of maps which Tasmanians carry on about but nobody listens.

"I've seen apples," I told him. "If I could afford a holiday, I would go somewhere where they have things I haven't seen."
"It wouldn't cost much," Geoffrey argued, "we could drive there."
"You mean I could drive there."
Geoffrey didn't own a car and caught the bus most places.

"They have a boat that ferries cars across. It costs... fifty-five dollars per vehicle under two tons. That's a bargain. How much does your car weigh?"

"Why would I know how much my car weighs?"

"Right. Hang on," he typed something into Alta Vista and waited patiently.

This was before Google was a thing. Or wi-fi. We had to plug a box into the telephone, run a cable to the computer, edit scripts so they would work with the box, try several different ppp settings, unplug the cables, plug them back in...

"We've got two flashing green lights on the modem now, what did you do?"

"I changed 255.255.182.4 to 255.255.182.5, hang on, I'll try 255.255.182.6"

"Three flashing green lights!"

"What do the flashing lights mean?"

"I'm not sure but three has to be better than two. Try changing it to 255.255.182.7... no, they're all off now."

Nowadays, everyone has Google on their phone and they can research information anywhere. It's practically impossible to make things up anymore without someone calling you out.

"Did you know that the word 'hike' originally comes from the time when the husband would ride on a mule while the wife had to walk alongside? As the routes were unpaved and

muddy, the wife would have to 'hike' up her skirt."
"That's not true, Google says it is comes from the old German word 'hyke' meaning 'to walk vigorously'."

"Ok," said Geoffrey, "It says here that a Fiat 124 Coupé weighs 2,205 pounds. That's around a ton. Even with our bags it will be well under the weight limit."

I'd traded up from my yellow 73' Honda hatchback after it broke in half while on the hoist at Ultra Tune getting the brake pads replaced. Apparently the chassis was completed rusted out and the front and back were only held together by the exhaust pipe. The green 75' Fiat seemed like an upgrade at the time but it was nowhere near as reliable. Due to something amiss with the electrical wiring, it would occasionally start itself and there was a coolant puddle in the driveway large enough that it needed to be leapt over.

"I doubt the Fiat would make it that far," I said, "it's only running on three cylinders and the radiator is shot."
"I'll pay for your car to be fixed and we can go halves in petrol. Motels are only about thirty dollars per night if you're not fussy about sleeping arrangements. If we go for a week the entire holiday will only cost a few hundred dollars. It will be a road trip."
"You'll pay to have my car fixed?"
"Yes."
"I don't actually have any assignments due."
"Excellent."

The drive from Adelaide to Melbourne, where we had to catch the ferry, took just over fourteen hours. It's an eight hour drive but we had to keep stopping to top up the radiator. Geoffrey's idea of paying to have the car fixed had consisted of purchasing a bottle of Wynn's Stop Leak and a new set of wiper blades.

"If we're going to be touring the 'apple isle' by car, we want a clean windshield to look out of. You don't have to pay me back for those. They were only four dollars."

As we missed the ferry by five hours and had to rebook for the next day, we spent that night in the ferry parking lot.

When the movie *The Mask* first came out, someone told Geoffrey that he did an excellent impression of the bit where Jim Carey says, "Smokin!" Since then, he'd wanted to be a voiceover artist, convinced that his repertoire of Fred Flintstone, Crocodile Dundee and John Cleese impressions were nothing short of a gift for others to experience. It was a very long night.

"This parrot is dead! He's an ex parrot. Bereft of life."
"Yes, I've seen it Geoffrey."
"No, you're meant to say, 'He's just resting.'"
"Can't we play I-spy instead?"
"Fine. I'll go first. I spy with my little eye, something beginning with an F."
"Well it's certainly not a ferry."

"No, but it's got the word ferry in it."

"What?"

"Yes, it's got three words."

"That's a sentence."

"No, it's a name. Of a place."

"Fuck that then, I'm not playing anymore. What was it?"

"Ferry Booking Office."

"I'm really tempted to drive the car off the edge of the dock right now and drown us both. What's the time?"

"11.15, so..." he counted off fingers, "eighteen hours and fifteen minutes until we get to board. You know what we should do?"

"What?"

"Hum parts of a song and the other person has to guess what the song is."

"I'm going to go to sleep."

"Oh no, don't do that. Then I'll be awake by myself and there's nothing to do. Come on, I'll start. Hmmm hmmm, hmm, hmmm hmmm hmm, hmm."

"Bohemian Rhapsody?"

"No. It didn't sound anything like Bohemian Rhapsody, you must be tone deaf. Here, I'll do it again. Hmm hmm, hmmm, hmm hmm hmm."

"That sounded completely different from the first time."

"That's because I did a different bit. That was the chorus. I'd have thought you'd get it easy with the chorus. Do you want me to hum it again?"

"No, I give it up. What was it?"

"*Don't You Want Me* by The Human League."

113

"What time is it now?"
"11.18."

At 4.30pm the next day, we were first in line to drive aboard. The ship was essentially a floating parking deck. Due to the booking change, the only tickets available were 'Ocean Recliner' which meant sitting in a chair overnight, with no shower facilities, after spending thirty-six hours in the car. A few chairs down from us, a couple had a child with a toothache and a set of healthy lungs but we managed to get a few minutes of sleep regardless. We drove off the ship into Devonport at 6.00 the next morning leaving a large puddle behind.

Devonport looked a lot like Adelaide and I had never been that impressed with Adelaide. We filled the radiator and headed south. Our original five day plan was to tour the island in a clockwise route with overnight stays in Launceston, Hobart, Queenstown and Burnie before arriving back in Devonport for departure. With only four days, we decided to bypass Launceston and head straight to Hobart.

"We should stop and buy apples," declared Geoffrey. We were driving through farming land and every few miles, kiosks selling apples were set up at the front of properties.
"Why?" I asked.
"We're in the Apple Isle. We have to buy apples. Tasmania

is famous for them. People will ask us about the apples when we get back and what are you going to tell them? That we didn't try any? That's just ridiculous."

"I'm fairly certain they are the same apples we buy in Adelaide. All our apples come from here."

"Yes, but these ones haven't been in a truck. And a boat. They're straight off the trees. Besides, we need snacks for the road trip. Pull over at this one."

Geoffrey purchased two large bags from the vendor, a woman with no teeth, who told us we were going in the wrong direction. We headed back the way we had come looking for the turnoff.

"Do you want one?" Geoffrey offered the bag to me.

"No thanks."

"You're not even going to try one?"

"I kind of like the green ones better. They're more crisp."

"These are pretty crisp," Geoffrey replied, "Listen..." he took a large bite.

"I stand corrected. That did indeed sound crisp."

"Do you want one then?"

"No thanks."

"Fine. All the more apples for me. I'm fairly sure that was the turnoff by the way."

"What?"

"You missed the turnoff."

"Well why didn't you tell me it was coming up?"

"You're the one driving."

"Yes, and you're the navigator," I countered, "That's your job. You have the map."

During our trip across on the ferry, we'd taken time out from our designated chairs to eat at the cafeteria. It was slim pickings, pre-wrapped sandwiches and the like, and we had to line up with trays like they make you do at IKEA. Our tray liners, an A3 piece of paper, featured an outline of Tasmania, with landmarks, for kids to colour in with a supplied small box of crayons. The crayons, four per box, were only slightly thicker than a piece of wire and one of them was white. They kept snapping and were constructed from a material not unlike crayon, but not similar enough to leave much of a mark on paper. Our proposed route was marked in purple crayon with tourist locations we intended to visit coloured in green. Geoffrey had also shaded the shoreline in with blue.

"The map doesn't show the turnoff. It just has a picture of a turtle. I'm going by what the old lady told me. She said to turn left at the big rock shaped like a boot. That road will take us to a main road that goes all the way to Hobart."
"Was there a rock shaped like a boot?"
"Kind of."
"Right. I'll keep going for a bit then and if we don't see a rock that is definitely shaped like a boot, we'll head back."
"No, it was definitely boot shaped."

I turned the car around and drove back. The rock wasn't

shaped anything like a boot.

"Maybe you misunderstood because of her thick Tasmanian accent and lack of teeth."

"No," Geoffrey replied, "She definitely said boot. Maybe it depends on which angle you look at it from."

"It's round. Whatever angle you look at it from, it's going to be round. Perhaps you should have asked her what kind of boot; a boot shaped one or the round kind."

"It's not perfectly round, it has a bit that sticks up at the back. I can definitely see a kind of boot shape."

We took the turnoff. It led to a farmhouse so we reversed back down their driveway and continued on along the highway until we found the correct landmark. It *was* actually shaped like a boot. Someone had spray-painted black laces on it. Someone else had spray-painted the words, 'Ken Matthews is a wanker' in white.

"Oh yes," said Geoffrey, "I saw that when we drove past earlier."

"You knew where the boot was?"

"It didn't register that it was boot-shaped at the time. I was too busy wondering who Ken Matthews is and if he has seen that rock. He would have been pretty cross."

On the five hour drive to Hobart, Geoffrey made me play a game that he invented called 'Number Plate People'. As cars drove past us, we had to record the letters and numerals from their number plate and use each letter as the first letters of someone's name. GZA-426 for example, became Glen Zoe Alice. The numbers indicated the probability of the person driving the car being called either Gen, Zoe or Alice. In this case, a 4 in 26 chance. It was far more excruciating than I am making it sound.

"Losing that day has really mucked up our schedule," Geoffrey complained as he marked our new route on the map. He'd tried colouring over the old route with the white crayon but it hadn't worked. He held it up. "Ignore everything in purple. Everything green is where we are going now. Except the green whale."

"Right, well you're the navigator. We've already established your skills in that area."

"Okay, because we lost a day, and it's now nearly noon on Sunday, we should turn left up here. That will take us to Port Arthur."

"What's at Port Arthur?"

"Its the ruins of an old prison."

"Oh good. I thought we were going straight to Hobart but visiting prison ruins sounds much better than food and a shower."

"We can eat at Port Arthur, "Geoffrey replied, "They have a cafe. If we go to Hobart first, we won't have to time to get there before the prison closes and I will have to colour over it with purple. I know how long it takes you to shower."

When I was growing up, my father had very strict water usage rules. If using the sink, under no circumstances were we to use the hot tap. If using the shower, we were not to exceed three minutes. He would set a timer and if the water was still on when the buzzer went off, he'd barge into the bathroom yelling and turn it off. He was a bit of a dick. As the shower took a few minutes to warm up, we had to lather ourselves with soap and shampoo outside the stream and use the remaining sixty seconds to wash it off. After my father left us, everyone took as long as they fucking wanted in the shower. Since then, my showers have extended to two, sometimes three, hours. I usually turn on the shower and make a coffee while waiting for it to get nice and steamy. Then I get in and have my coffee with a cigarette. After enjoying the water for a while, I shave, brush my teeth, shampoo my hair and wash. In that order but the time between each varies. Then I enjoy the water for a while. Sometimes I try to drown a bug or see how much water I can hold with my arms crossed or hold my arms down with my fingers splayed to make the water run off the tips. My current bathroom has a television and coffee machine in it. I tried putting a bean bag in the shower but after a few months, the stitching rotted away and it burst so now I use a camping chair.

The Port Arthur Historical Site was an hour out of our way. Geoffrey suggested we continue our game of Number Plate People and I threatened to swerve into oncoming traffic.

"Let's play 'Science Fiction movies' then. I'll say a science fiction movie and whatever letter it ends with, you have to name a science fiction movie that starts with that letter."

"Righto," I agreed, "*Star Wars.*"

"No, I go first."

"Okay."

"*Star Wars.*"

"Really? Fine. *Star Wars, The Empire Strikes Back.*"

"No, you can't use *Star Wars* twice in a row."

"Are you just saying that because you can't think of a science fiction film that starts with K?" I asked.

"No."

"Fine, *Spaceballs* then."

"That's really more of a comedy than science fiction, but I'll let you have it. *Star Wars, The Empire Strikes Back.*"

"Right, I'm not playing anymore."

"Oh come on."

"No. I wouldn't have thought it possible ten minutes ago, but you actually managed to come up with a game more painful than Number Plate People."

"Let's play Animals then."

"Do you name an animal and I use the last letter to name another animal?"

"No," I make an animal sound and you have to guess what it is. I'll go first. Araack!"

"That just sounded like someone yelling the name Eric. Is it Eric's mother?"

"No, it's Araack!, not Eric. I'll give you a clue, it's brown."

"That's not much of a clue. Most animals are brown."

"Yes, but only one of them says Araack!"

"Is it a camel?"

"No."

I give up then. What was it?

"Oh don't give up yet," Geoffrey moaned, "I'll give you one more clue. It has long eyelashes."

"That's all I get to go on? It's brown, has long eyelashes, and yells Eric?"

"Araack!"

"Right, well I don't give a fuck what it is, it sounds dreadful."

"It was a seal.

"It didn't sound anything like a seal. Seals bark."

"No, that's dogs. Because you didn't get it, I get to go again. Braaad!"

We arrived and drove through a toll booth and into the parking lot just after 1pm. It was a nice day, warm with blue skies and a light breeze. There were quite a few tourists. Geoffrey consulted the brochure we had been given.

"What do you want to look at first? The prison ruins or the church ruins?"

"Where's the cafe?" I asked.

Geoffrey consulted the brochure again. It had a little map on the back. He pointed to a building.

"That's the gift shop and cafe," he said, "but we should look at the ruins first. I'm not really all that hungry."

"Really? You only ate two bags of apples. You don't want a barrel of plums or a bucket of apricots to go with them? I'm going to get something to eat."

We made our way up the steps of the building and entered through the gift shop. I bought a black and white striped t-shirt with 'Inmate of Port Arthur Prison' written on it. Geoffrey bought a coffee mug and a fridge magnet.

The cafe had the IKEA tray system so we grabbed a tray each and made our way down the line. I had my eye on a cherry danish but the man in front of us took it.

"Good choice," I said, "I was going to get that."
The man turned and frowned. He had blonde wavy hair, parted in the middle, and was carrying a big bag.
"You can have it if you like. It's burnt on the edges. I don't like them when they are overcooked."
He offered the danish to me.
"No, no. You enjoy your cherry danish. I'm sure it will be delicious despite the burnt edges."
"I don't mind."
"I'll have it then," said Geoffrey. He took the danish.
The man with the blonde wavy hair and I both selected a slice of carrot cake instead.
"Snap." I said.
"What?"
"Snap. You know, the card game."
"No. Is it like Uno?"
"Not really."

"It's more like Go Fish," Geoffrey interjected helpfully.

"No, it's not," I told the man with blonde wavy hair, "Don't listen to him. He's insane."

"It's for the same age group," Geoffrey argued.

"Right, so by that argument, Slip'n'Slide is also similar to Snap."

"I've never played Slip Inside so I wouldn't know," said Geoffrey, "Is it like Go Fish?"

"Are you serious? Slip'n'Slide. The long piece of yellow plastic that you put on your lawn, spray water on, and kids slide down."

"Oh, you mean the Splash'n'Ride'?"

"What the fuck? Who calls it the Splash'n'Ride?"

"That's what the one we had was called."

"You must have had a cheap Chinese knockoff then, the real one is called Slip'n'Slide. Where'd you get it?"

"I'm not sure. Maybe Target. Can you pass me one of those Splades please?"

Further up the line, I added a cheese sandwich and a bag of chips to my tray. Geoffrey selected a banana to "mix things up a bit." I have no idea what the man with the blonde wavy hair added because Geoffrey and I were busy arguing whether the plastic spoons with a built-in fork were called splades or sporks. We paid for our meal and made our way outside to eat on the balcony. Wasps hovered near an open bin by the door so I carried on a bit and we sat at a table towards the back. I'm not a fan of wasps.

Once when I was young, my family drove up the coast to stay at a beachside town called Kalbari during summer break. We rented a cabin at the Kalbarri Caravan Park. On the beach, there was a small shack that rented out snorkelling equipment so my sister and I hurriedly searched through bags for our swimming outfits. My father walked around with his hands on his hips, nodding and commenting on what an excellent choice in accommodation he had made.

"Look, ceiling fans. Very nice. The ceiling appears to be bowing here though, and there's a stain in the middle that looks wet."

He reached up on tippy toes and poked the wet spot with his finger. His finger went straight through, opening a hole about an inch in diameter. Wasps poured out of the hole. Thousands of them. The room looked like yellow and black static. Everyone was stung multiple times but my father took the brunt of the attack. After he was released from hospital, my mother had to drive the car home because my father couldn't open his eyes due to the swelling. It was the third worst holiday I have ever been on.

The man with the blonde wavy hair sat a few tables down from us. He smiled and raised his spork with a bit of carrot cake on it as way of a salute.

"They're not European wasps so you don't have to worry," he said.

"Sorry?"

"Those are just normal wasps. There's a lot of wasps about today but I haven't seen any European wasps."

"What's the difference?" Geoffrey asked, seemingly quite interested, "Is there a noticeable size or colour variation?" The man with the blonde wavy hair seemed pleased at this engagement.

"They're the same colour but European wasps are smaller than normal wasps. They look more like bees. A man came to our house and hung European wasp traps on the trees in our backyard because our neighbour's had a nest of them in their shed. I looked in one and it was full of dead European wasps. We've got lots of European wasps in Tasmania but those," he indicated towards the bin, "are just Yellow Paper Wasps. They won't kill you."

"Well that's good to hear," said Geoffrey, "You certainly know a lot about wasps."

"That's because I'm a wasp scientist," said the man with the blonde curly hair, "that's my job."

"Really?" I asked, "Why didn't you put the traps on the trees yourself then?"

Geoffrey kicked my leg under the table.

"It's a valid question," I continued, "Had you run out of your own wasp traps? As a wasp scientist, it might be assumed that you'd have an abundant supply."

"So," said Geoffrey, attempting to change the subject, "you live around here then? That must be nice."

"Apart from all the wasps of course," I added, "You'll probably be on top of that though once you get some more traps."

Geoffrey kicked me again.

The man with the blonde curly hair nodded, "Are you from the mainland?"

"Yes," Geoffrey answered, finishing the last bite of his banana, "Adelaide. It's a shithole."

Adelaide isn't a shithole. It has some nice bits. It's the people that live in Adelaide that ruin it. Seen as a kind of joke by the rest of Australia, Adelaidians spend a lot of their time trying to convince themselves, and other Adelaidians, that they are not a joke and are actually fairly damn awesome. This means dressing in the latest European fashions, even just to visit the supermarket, and pretending they spend a lot of time in Melbourne and Sydney. Adelaide is more like a large village than a city. A village where the idiots outnumber normal townsfolk a hundred to one and they all wear G-Star and Diesel. The tourism slogan for Adelaide is, *It's Heaps Good*. I wish I was making this up.

We left our trays on a counter near the bins, dodged a few wasps, and wandered down a grassy hill towards the ruins. Behind us, the man with the blonde wavy hair finished his meal and carried his big bag back inside the cafe.

"I've never met a wasp scientist before," I said to Geoffrey, "I certainly learnt a lot."

"He seemed harmless enough," Geoffrey replied, "You have to expect Tasmanians to be a little odd. They don't have much to do apart from growing apples so they probably get a bit bored and make up stories to sound more interesting. Stand on top of that rock and I'll take a photo."

When I was nine, I told a kid at school that I was having a birthday party and he could come if he wanted. It was nowhere near my birthday, I just made the whole thing up. The kid was kind of a bully and I thought that by inviting him, he would direct his attention towards others. Word quickly got around and, cornered by the lie, I confirmed to around twenty kids that yes, I was having a birthday party and yes, they could come. I was enjoying the attention at this stage. To add realism, I provided each a sheet from a pad of party invites with my address and a date set weeks in the future figuring this would give me enough time to think of a way out of the whole thing. I forgot all about it until the first guests arrived. My father was watching cricket on television while my mother was out doing the weekly shopping.

"I'll stand next to it," I said to Geoffrey, "there's no point standing on it. People are watching."
"Just stand on it." he replied, "How is standing *next* to a rock even remotely interesting? We should make it our theme."
"Our theme?"
"Yes, the theme of our holiday photos. We stand on a rock in every shot. Oh, no..."
"What?"
"We should have got a photo standing on the rock shaped like a boot."

'Yes," I agreed, "and the round one."

Geoffrey frowned, "No, that would be stupid."

I stood on the rock.

"Okay," Geoffrey queried, "is that what you are going to do? Just stand there? You don't want to pretend you're doing something?"

"Like what?"

"I don't know, pointing at something perhaps."

"No, just take the photo."

"What if you jumped with your arms in the air."

"Like an action shot?"

"Yes, exactly."

"No, just take the photo."

Inside the café, the man with the blonde wavy hair unzipped his big bag, took out an AR-15 semi-automatic assault rifle, and began shooting patrons and staff.

"Gunshots!" exclaimed Geoffrey, "We're missing a reenactment. I bet a convict has escaped and the prison wardens are chasing him. Let's go watch."

"It's coming from way up the hill." I replied, "We just came from there. They will probably do another one in an hour. Let's just finish looking at rocks and then we can walk back up. It sounds like it's finished anyway."

The man with the blonde wavy hair reloaded the assault rifle and stepped out of the cafe. Tourists heading towards the area hoping to catch part of a reenactment were fired upon.

"No," said Geoffrey, "Listen, it's still going. Quick, take a photo of me standing on the rock and then we'll go watch." Geoffrey climbed onto the rock, looked to his left and held his hand to his forehead.

"Why are you saluting?" I asked.

"I'm not," he replied, "I'm gazing into the distance. Just hurry up and take the shot. We're missing the reenactment."

"Ok," I took the photo, "Now, put your hands on your knees, bend them a little, turn to the side a bit, a bit more, and put your head back and smile..."

"You really are a dickhead," Geoffrey said, jumping down.

We were half way back up the hill when an old lady came running down past us. She was a large woman with blue eyeshadow, a tight perm and tighter white slacks. Both her knees had large green grass stains where she had fallen and skidded.

"Run!" she screamed.

We ran. The look on her face as she yelled her warning was all the convincing we needed.

"Is it zombies?" Geoffrey yelled as we passed her.

Many hours later, after police officers took our statements and contact information, we were free to leave. We hadn't been anywhere near the cafe during the shootings so could provide no helpful eyewitness accounts. There was no discussion about driving back to Devonport, I just drove there. Both of us wanted to be home.

"I hope the wasp guy is alright," said Geoffrey.
"I'm sure he's fine," I said, "I didn't see him... you know."
Geoffrey nodded, "They were covered though. It was pretty hard to tell. Some of the sheets were small..."
"Do you want to play Number Plate People?" I asked.
"Alright."

Sarah's Arms

My offspring told me a joke recently. Most of his jokes are terrible and I usually just say 'ha' after the punchline as a half-hearted nod to the effort.

"Why did Sarah fall off the swing?" Seb asked.
"I don't know, why?"
"Because she had no arms."
I was pretty disappointed at this and didn't feel it deserved a 'ha' so I just said, "hm."
"Knock knock." Seb said.
"Fine. Who's there?"
"Not Sarah."

Seb and I both laughed for a bit and I went back to ordering a fish pond pump on Amazon and he went back to yelling at his friends online. He plays the Modern Black Ops a lot. Sometimes when Seb is in Australia and I'm in the United States, I'll suggest we play the Modern Black Ops and he tells me that if I am not going to bother learning what the game is really called, then he's not going to waste his time explaining to me how to connect to Xbox Love again. I told the same joke to Holly a few hours later while she was making nachos.

"Why did Sarah fall off the swing?"

"Who's Sarah?" Holly asked.

"That doesn't matter. Why did she fall off the swing?"

"Why are you asking me? I don't know anybody named Sarah. If it was the swing at the park it's probably because the equipment is fifty years old. Did it break or was she just being careless? Is she alright?"

"No," I answered, "she died. You know how when you are a kid and your friends dare you to get a good speed up and perform a full 360 flip around the bar? She lost her grip mid-rotation and was thrown almost twenty feet over the fence and onto the road. A FedEx truck ran over her."

"That seems pretty unlikely. Are you making this up?"

"Yes," I told her, "it's a joke. I'll start again. Just say 'I don't know' when I ask why Sarah fell off the swing ok?"

"Fine."

"Right, so, why did Sarah fall off the swing?"

"Because she tried to do a 360 degree flip?" Holly answered hopefully.

"No, what? No, it was because she had no arms."

Holly just stared at me so I added, "Hahaha."

"That's the joke?" she asked, "She has no arms? I saw a show on television last week about a girl who was born without arms or legs and she was able to do almost everything the other kids at school did. She just wanted to be treated like everyone else. What if we have a baby that is born without any arms? Will that be funny? I'll be thirty soon and the older you are, the higher the chance of these things happening."

"Knock knock."

132

"What?"

"Just ask who it is," I told her, "Knock knock."

"Who is it?"

"Not Sarah."

"Hahaha," I added.

Holly frowned thoughtfully, "She could easily knock with her feet or hold something in her mouth and knock with that. There is a local artist that paints by holding a brush in his mouth and his work is amazing."

"I've seen his work," I replied, "and it is only deemed amazing because he paints with a brush in his mouth. If his work stood on its own, he wouldn't need to advertise the fact that he hasn't got any arms."

"Why do you hate people with no arms so much?"

"I don't. There is a famous monkey that paints and everyone says 'that's pretty good for a monkey.' It's the same thing. If a human produced the same calibre of work as that monkey, nobody would care. That doesn't mean I hate monkeys. "

"You do hate monkeys."

"Yes, but not because of their artwork. They have lice."

"What if," suggested Holly, "a monkey with no arms painted a picture with a brush in its mouth? You have to admit that would be pretty impressive."

"Yes, for a monkey without arms. It doesn't mean I would want the picture on my wall."

"Well I better hope I never lose my arms."

"Or turn into a monkey."

"Now you're just being an idiot," Holly said scoldingly, "Why would I turn into a monkey?"

"I don't know. Some kind of science experiment where you wake up to find yourself with the same thoughts but in the body of a monkey. Why would you lose your arms?"

"People lose their arms all the time. I could be in an accident or I could get attacked by a shark or something. We are booked for a week at the beach next month with my parents, would you still love me if a shark bit off both my arms?"

"Of course I would but as you spend the entire time under an umbrella drinking margaritas, I would be a lot more impressed by the sharks ability to walk up the beach and take your arms than a monkey dabbing randomly at a piece of paper with a brush."

"What if I did wake up in the body of a monkey," asked Holly, "Would you still love me then?"

"Do you have arms?"

"No."

"Well it might put a bit of a strain on the relationship but I'm sure we could work through it. People would see us at the supermarket and say, 'There's David and his armless monkey wife. Love certainly can overcome all."

"God you are a liar." she said, "Well it's good to know these things about someone before they happen I suppose."

"What things?"

"That you hate people with no arms."

"I don't hate people with no arms. It was a joke."

"Well," Holly replied, "perhaps you should leave the jokes to people who are funny. You're not Freddy Murphy."

Traditions

I'm not a huge fan of the beach. When I lived in Australia, I was only ever a half hour drive away but I rarely went. Occasionally my offspring would want to go but I'd tell him the beach was closed that day or give him a choice between going to the beach or cash. When I was young, every family trip to the beach either ended in somebody being hurt or my parents fighting so it became something to avoid rather than look forward to.

Where I currently live in the United Sates with my wife Holly, the nearest beach is several hour's drive away. This makes avoiding going to the beach on a regular basis easier but it also means, for my wife Holly and her parents at least, the annual family week at the beach is a big deal. Every year, since Holly was a small child, her parents have booked a beach house at a place called Emerald Isle in North Carolina. Last summer, for months leading up to the trip, it was all her father talked about.

"Only eighty-three days 'till we'll be sitting on a chair at the beach; are you excited? I can't wait. I bought a new fold-up chair from Home Depot. It has a built-in drink holder on the arm rest. My old fold-up chair didn't have that. It's blue. They only had green and blue."

Family traditions are nice. They're a way of ensuring time is spent together on a regular basis, regardless of where each member of the family is in their life. I didn't have any family traditions growing up, unless avoiding each other counts. My first family tradition was when Holly and I bought a tree for our first Christmas together in the United States. In Australia, December is hot. It's the middle of summer and temperatures reach scorching levels. Once, it reached 54° Celsius which I think in Imperial is 425° Fahrenheit or 11/16ths of a Cubit. Christmas is celebrated to a degree but songs about dashing through snow hold no relevance. Children's books show Santa wearing shorts and families spend Christmas Eve in front of an air conditioner rather than a roaring Yuletide log. It snowed on my first Christmas in America, like it does in the movies, and Holly and I visited a Christmas tree farm. In long coats, with a dusting of light snow on our shoulders, we walked for over an hour among fir trees comparing height and foliage density.

"This one! It's perfect! I love it!" Holly exclaimed.
"It's at least fifteen feet tall. Our ceilings are about eight."
"God dammit. I knew we should have bought a bigger house."
"We could cut it in half and just use the top bit," I suggested.
"No, let someone with a nice house have it. We'll just take the sticky one you liked."

An old man wearing flannel and denim cut the sticky one down for us with a chainsaw and tied it to the roof of our car. On the way home, the rope slipped and we dragged the tree along the freeway for a quarter mile or so until we could pull over to secure it. Later, we positioned the side without any branches against a wall and after Holly decorated it with forty strings of lights, several hundred baubles and a skirt, the tree wasn't really visible anyway.

"It looks good but what's that thing around the bottom?"
"It's a tree skirt."
"Is that an American thing? What's it for?"
"To hide the tree stand. And look nice."
"Does it need the skirt?"
"You don't like it?"
"It's just a bit big. It looks like the Christmas tree is standing in the middle of a really big rug. A really big round rug with snowmen and Santas dancing together on it. It's not the kind of rug we'd usually have in the living room."
"We wouldn't usually have a fucking tree in the living room either. It's Christmas."
"I like the tree. And the red stockings on the mantel and the laurel with the red bow on the door, but do we need a giant Christmas rug? It's a bit, I don't know, goodwilly."
"Goodwilly?"
"Yes, like it came from a Goodwill store. It's the fabric I think. And the pattern. And the size.
"Fine. Sorry for trying to make it festive around here. Maybe we should take down all the other decorations as well. Actually, I don't even want to have Christmas anymore. Thanks for ruining Christmas, Uncle Scrooge."

"The duck?"

"No, the grumpy old man that made Tiny Tim sell matches on Christmas Eve. You really need to read the classics."

The day before we were due to leave for the beach, we packed our vehicle with bags, chairs, cooler and an inflateable killer whale. I'd gone shopping for beach attire a few days earlier and bought my very first hat and a pair of 'flip-flops' - which are called 'thongs' in Australia.

"Marjorie, this gentleman wants to know if we sell black rubber thongs. For men."

"No. He will probably have to try a sex shop."

"That's what I told him."

I'm not a hat person so when I tried my Indiana Jones fedora on later at home, I paraded in front of a mirror for about an hour before deciding it looked pretty good. I tried the hat with my new flip-flops and was pleased with the combination. I threw them in a bag with a pair of boardshorts and a couple of t-shirts and was done. Holly packed three large suitcases. Two were for shoes.

Holly's parents drove their own car because they had to take their cats. Cats love the beach and long drives. One of them died on the way. There were tears. After we arrived at the beach house that night, Holly's father Tom gave 'Bob' a service and burial by flashlight. Holly's mother Marie realised she didn't have a photo of Bob so before Tom shovelled sand into the hole, she took a close-up flash shot of his face.

The beach house was nice. It was well-appointed and had a wraparound deck. We sat outside listening to the waves crash in the darkness while Tom talked about what a good cat Bob had been and Marie quoted something she had read about dead cats sitting on a brightly coloured bridge waiting for you to die and join them. I went to bed early.

The next morning, Holly and I woke before her parents and had coffee on the deck. Neighbouring beachhouse occupants were already setting their umbrellas up on the beach and two boys were building a sand castle. One dug up Bob and chased the other with him.

"Oh my god. Is that Bob?" asked Holly.
"Yes. I knew your dad should have dug a deeper hole."
"He tried but the sand kept falling back in. What are they doing with him?"
"They're chasing and throwing him at each other."
"Well do something about it."
"They're having fun."
"Go down there and take it off them. And do it quick, my parents will be up soon."

I made my way down to the beach and recovered the dead cat from the boys. Looking towards the beach house and raising the cat in triumph, I saw Holly frantically pointing to the sliding door behind her. Thinking her parents might step out onto the deck any second, I threw the cat into the ocean. I'd assumed it would sink but instead, it caught the first wave and bodysurfed straight back in. I quickly searched around for a decent sized rock, secured it under the cat's collar and threw it out again. Bob bobbed for a moment then sank head first, his tail pointing up like the stern of the Titanic before disappearing. On my way back up to the beach house, I kicked over the sandcastle and leveled the sand with my foot.

Holly's mother, Marie, made pancakes for breakfast. I didn't eat any because I saw one of the surviving cats jump up on the counter and lick the batter bowl while she was making them. I'm pretty much against cats being on kitchen counters, or in the house, or anywhere in general. I pretended I wasn't hungry and ate a Snicker's bar in the bathroom.

After breakfast, Tom and I carried gear down to the beach and set up the umbrella while Holly and her mother went to buy ice from a 7-Eleven. I was wearing my new outfit and feeling pretty good about it.

"Is that a new hat?" Tom asked.
"Yes, it's a Fedora."
"That's not a Fedora, a Fedora is a little hat without a brim. Like a flower pot. Except it has a tassel on the top. You see guys driving around in little cars during parades wearing them."
"You mean a Fez?"

"A what?"

"It's called a Fez."

"Is it? Well you need to get yourself a cap like mine," Tom said, "It's got ventilation."

He took off his blue trucker cap and pointed out the mesh.

"See? You lose ninety-nine percent of your body heat through your head. Your Fez is going to trap all of that heat and make you sweat. The mesh serves a double purpose - it lets the breeze through and the heat out."

"I doubt that it's ninety-nine percent," I replied, "It's probably closer to thirty. Which is still a lot seeing as the top of your head probably only accounts for about three percent of total surface area."

"No, it's ninety-nine percent. Heat rises. You're going to sweat."

"Yes, probably, but you know, form over function."

"What?"

"Form over function. It's a design thing. I'll put up with a sweaty head because I like the hat."

"You should put slits in it. For ventilation. I've got a knife in the cooler somewhere for cutting limes... here it is. Pass me your hat."

"No thanks."

"You don't want ventilation? You need ventilation. Keeps your head cool."

"Yes, I understand the concept, I just don't want you to stab holes in my new hat."

Tom opened his Alcatel flip-phone and punched in numbers.

"Marie? It's Tom. Are you at the 7-Eleven yet? Okay, as you go through the door, to your right, there's a shelf with caps on it. The ones with mesh on the sides. Get one of those for David. He needs ventilation."

"No I don't, Marie," I shouted, "I'm fine."

"Blue I guess," Tom continued, "No? Hang on," he turned to me, "There's no blue, would you prefer red or green?"

"Neither. I've already got a hat."

"Marie? Just grab the green one.... no, it doesn't matter what it says on it... Okay, bye."

Even though it was early we had a beer because Tom wanted to try out the built-in drink holder on the arm of his new foldup chair. He took off his shirt and moved his chair into the sun. I plugged a foot pump into the inflateable killer whale and began pumping. I haven't pumped a lot of things up in my life. I'd assumed it would take thirty or forty pumps.

"You haven't got that pumped up yet?" asked Holly when she and Marie returned.

"Yes," I answered, "but it was so enjoyable, I deflated it so I could pump it back up again. I'm actually on my third go."

"Here's your hat, David," said Marie.

She passed me a green cap with 'I'd Rather Be Fishing' written across the front. I glanced at Holly, she avoided eye contact.

I have no interest in fishing whatsoever. I've only ever been fishing twice. Once with Greg Norman and a guy who rollerskated in Xanadu, and once with my friend Geoffrey many years before. Geoffrey had borrowed his father's small dinghy and fishing gear and we launched, mid morning, in a small bay protected from large waves by outer reefs. He rowed around a bit for no particular reason and we threw the anchor over. The first few minutes of fishing were ok. It became a bit boring after that.

"I should have bought Scrabble." I said to Geoffrey.
"Fishing is about relaxing," he told me, "Take your top off and get a tan."
"I might just do that actually. It's very sunny and nobody is going to see me out here."
We both took our tops off and made ourselves comfortable at opposite ends of the dinghy.
"I should have brought a hat," I commented.
"What hat? I've never seen you wearing a hat."
"No, I'm not big on hats. I should buy one though. For fishing on sunny days. Maybe a Fedora."
"A sombrero would work a lot better."
"Would you wear a sombrero?"
"No."
"Well there you go then. I should have brought a hat and Scrabble. Or my Sony Walkman."
Geoffrey dug around in a pocket of his cargo shorts, "I bought a joint."

I'm not sure if it was strong marijuana or a combination of the marijuana, sun, and how boring fishing is, but we both fell asleep. Geoffrey woke me five hours later by yelling. I bolted upright and also yelled. From our knees down and waist up, we were both scarlet red. Yellow blisters had formed and some popped, leaking clear fluid, as I watched. We sat at each end of the dinghy sobbing with our arms outstretched.

"Is it on my face?"

"Yes, is it on my face too?" It hurt to speak.

"Yes. Can you bend your arms?"

I tried, "Ahhh. No."

"How are we going to row back?"

"Maybe we could swim," I suggested, "Or you could swim and bring back help."

"I'm not swimming. There's sharks in there."

"There's people on the beach, maybe we can get their attention."

We both tried waving, wincing at the pain.

"No," Geoffrey said sadly, "We're too far away. We're going to have to row. Help me pull up the anchor."

With a lot of complaining, we managed to pull the anchor over the side and took an oar each. It was excruciating to bend so we used the oars as paddles. Geoffrey dropped his and we had to let it go so we took it in turns with one. We didn't cover much distance and we needn't have bothered as a larger fishing boat came past and rescued us a few hours later. They radioed ahead to have an ambulance waiting. Due to a communication error about picking up two sunburnt and dehydrated fishermen that had obviously been drifting for days, possibly weeks, there was also a couple of reporters with cameras from the local news station waiting. We were on the news that night, the video clip showed Geoffrey and I being loaded into an ambulance on stretchers. A reporter asked Geoffrey how long we had been adrift at sea and Geoffrey answered, "All day."

We were in the hospital for a week, covered head to toe in Vaseline. They put us in the same room though so it wasn't all bad; Geoffrey invented a game where he would tap randomly on his bedrail and I had to guess which television commercial it was.

"Here, give me a go," said Holly. She pumped three or four times then squeezed the inflateable killer whale to see if it had gotten any bigger.
"Okay, you take over," she said.
"Try on your cap." Tom called out, "Your head must be getting pretty sweaty with all that pumping."
"Yes, thank you Tom, I might try it on later this afternoon. When the beach clears a bit."
Holly glared. "You'll hurt their feelings," she whispered, "That cap cost twenty dollars."
"You wear it then."
"Just put it on. And pretend you like it. I'll scratch your back for ten minutes later."
"No."
"Fifteen minutes."
"Fine."

Back scratches are a form of currency in our house. They range from five minutes for emptying the kitchen bin to thirty minutes for attending work functions or doing the vacuuming. Both Holly and I hate doing the vacuuming. We bought one of those little robot vacuum cleaners called an iRobot but what they don't show you in the commercials is all the banging into furniture and beeping when it gets stuck. You also have to pick everything up off the floor before it runs and clean it out every time it's finished. It takes it about two hours to clean an average sized room. I'd rather suck the dust up with a straw than listen to the horrible thing whirring around banging and beeping for two hours. If we leave the house with it running, it manages to clean approximately four square inches before getting stuck. Once we found it upside down and another time it disappeared for a week when we left the back door ajar.

"Actually," I said to Tom, "My head *is* getting a bit sweaty." I took off my Fedora and put on the cap.
"I told you it would," he replied, "It looks good. Very high. It makes your face look longer. No, don't try to push it down, you need that extra space for good ventilation."
"It *does* have good ventilation," I admitted, "You were right about that. Plus now everyone will know that I would rather be fishing without me having to tell them."
"You can wear it gardening," Marie added helpfully.
"That's true, I should plant some corn."

I went back to pumping. One of the fins on the inflateable

killer whale filled out a bit.

"Try pumping it faster," Holly suggested.

Twenty minutes later, the inflateable killer whale was still only partially inflated. I declared the pump faulty and continued the job by mouth. Tom fed Cheetos to seagulls, Marie repeated her story about colourful bridges because she had forgotten the bit about the cats being able to talk, and Holly kept a running commentary on how inflated the killer whale wasn't.

Tom removed his cap and kicked off his flip flops.

"I'm going for a swim," he declared, "Are you coming in Marie?"

"No," Marie replied, "I had some of your Cheetos so I should wait half an hour."

"Cheetos don't count," said Tom.

"It's better to be safe than sorry," answered Marie.

"Fine. Holly?"

"In a minute," Holly replied, "I'm waiting to take the inflateable killer whale in. It's going up pretty quickly now."

Tom headed down to the water. A wave crashed and ran up the sand to cover his feet.

"It's warm," he called back to us.

He walked forward until he was up to knees.

"It's like bath water."

"Is the tide coming in or going out?" I asked Holly.

"Out I think, why?" Her eyes widened.

Tom took a few steps deeper. He stopped, peering at something just below the surface. Reaching under, he pulled Bob out by the tail. Two crabs were attached to Bob's face.

"Who would have done this?" Tom asked horrified. He cradled Bob like a baby. One of the crabs had fallen off, Tom had beaten the other off with a flip-flop. Most of Bob's face was missing. "Someone threw him in the ocean on purpose, look, there's a rock under his collar to weigh him down!"

Holly looked at me. Tom and Marie looked at me. I was a bit annoyed at Holly for that; if she hadn't given me away, I would have been able to feign outrage that someone would do such a thing and say, "It was probably kids. You know what kids are like."

"He wouldn't sink," I explained.

There was a lot more yelling than listening after that. Things were said. Things about appropriate social behaviour and things about appropriate grave depths. Marie cried and went back up to the beachhouse, Holly chased after her. Tom threw my Fedora into the ocean. I threw Tom's new folding chair with the built-in cup holder into the ocean. He picked up the knife he had brought to cut limes. For a few seconds, I actually thought he was going to stab me. I'm pretty sure there was a moment where he at least considered it, even though he has told me since that he didn't.

"No, don't!" I yelled, stepping back. My fight or flight response is definitely geared towards the later.

Tom stabbed the inflateable killer whale. Three or four times. It was exactly like the shower scene in Psycho. Except with a big 'pop' instead of screaming and it was sunny and we were wearing well ventilated caps. He then kicked over the cooler, emptying the contents onto the sand, placed Bob inside, and closed the lid.

"Thanks for ruining the family holiday," he said and stormed up to the beach house carrying the cooler.

I tried to find his chair by walking around in the water feeling with my feet, but, knowing there were crabs in the water, I didn't try very hard. I did find my fedora though so that was lucky. Holly's parents packed their belongings, cats and the cooler into their car and left. Holly and I left an hour or so after them.

I visited Home Depot a few weeks later to buy Tom a replacement chair. They'd run out of blue, so I got him a green one. He still wasn't talking to me so I quietly left it on the front porch by the door. The cooler was also on the porch so I cracked the lid and peeked inside just to make sure Bob wasn't still in there.

"We buried him," said Tom. I hadn't heard him open the door.

"Oh," I said, startled, "Where?"

Toms eyes narrowed, "I'm not telling you."

This summer, I tentatively asked Tom if he'd booked a beach house for this year and he told me that he and Marie had decided to spend the money on a gazebo for their backyard instead.

Short Men

I knew my neighbour Carl was going to be trouble the first time I met him. He's a short man and short men are angry, horrible things. Being born short is something a woman can live with - it's seen as cute - but a short man will never forgive the world for such a cruel blow. Short men hate normal sized humans, they wish cancer and car accidents against them and have dreams about being the size of a mountain and stomping on people. Short men have short fat wives with tight curly hair and they are angry about this as well.

We purchased our property when the trees were in full bloom. It's a nice, unpretentious place with a wraparound deck on a few private wooded acres with trails and a river nearby.

I've never owned a house before. The day Holly and I signed a foot high stack of documents and were given the keys, we drove to our new property and walked from room to room discussing what we would do to the place. It wasn't a new home, it was built in the eighties and had certain design elements pertaining to that period. People really liked glass bricks in the eighties. And pastels. And carpet with flecks that looks like someone has spun around in circles while holding an open box of cake sprinkles.

"We have to paint first," said Holly.

Every room was a different colour or technique. The previous owner must have watched one of those DIY shows where they show you how to sponge paint onto a wall to create a textured effect but missed the part apart using shades of the same colour. The base colour in the living room was battleship grey, the highlight lemon yellow. It looked like someone had thrown custard at an elephant.

"Then we'll put in floorboards, rip out the kitchen and bathrooms, and make the master bedroom bigger. With a large walk-in closet. For me. You can get a set of drawers or something."

"That will cost a fortune" I said.

"They don't have to be good drawers, ones from IKEA or something."

"No, the renovations will be expensive."

"No they won't. We'll do all the work ourselves. We've watched a thousand home renovation shows."

"Yes, but the people in the show have a show because they know what they are doing."

"Not really. That blonde lady that buys the old houses and does them up is just winging it and her stuff turns out alright."

"The one that says, 'Why the hell would they cover that up" at the start of each episode? I like that show."

"You love her, don't you?"

We painted the walls (Valspar silver dust) and the house looked a lot better. Encouraged, we tackled a bathroom. Enthused, we did another bathroom and the kitchen. Then the floors. Holly mainly supervised. Her expertise lay in complaining about dust and asking why I didn't hang up plastic sheets before doing dusty things. She could use a screwdriver when she had to but pretended to be incapable of operating power tools.

"What's the NO button for?
"What?"
"The button that says NO."
"You're holding it upside down."

My friend JM was very helpful though. He's a builder by trade so whenever I completed each project, he'd visit to tell me what a terrible job I'd done.

"Did you check if that wall is load bearing?"
"Well, no, but..."
"The entire roof is going to collapse and you're going to die. Also, remember to change your smoke alarm batteries every six months, the rewiring you did in the kitchen is a tragedy waiting to happen. Have you ever been in a house fire?"
"No."
"You will be."

I knocked out walls, added walls, stole space from other rooms for walk in closets, stained the deck, added to the deck, stained that. For six months, I lived in cargo shorts, knee-pads and sturdy boots. I wore a measuring tape on my belt and my pockets were full of drill bits and carpenter pencils. I knew the names of all the staff at my local hardware store and purchased every tool they stocked.

"David, didn't see you yesterday."
"Well I was here. You must have been working in the shelving aisle. I was in plumbing. How's Brenda and the baby doing?"
"They're good. What are you getting today?"
"I actually just came in for a hinge but I'll grab this reticulating saw, orbital sander, bench grinder, air compressor, extension cord and 36 pack of AA batteries as well."

Then the money ran out.

What's this charge on Visa for six-hundred dollars?"
"From which day?"
"Tuesday."
"That would be the Oxy-Acetylene welder then."
"What are you welding?"
"Nothing, it's just handy to have."
"You're taking it back."

I was like a junkie without means to my next hit. For a few days, I wandered aimlessly about the house staring at walls that needed doors in them and doors that needed to be walls - possibly with some kind of rustic faux-brick application.

I measured things and nodded sadly. I stopped watching the DIY channel, it was like watching porn with both your arms amputated.

"Why don't you do some work outside?" Holly suggested.
"Hm."
"You could build a pond."

Plans were drawn, shovels sharpened, the recommended water depth for Koi researched.

Digging the hole took longer than I'd anticipated. The soil was compacted and there were a lot of rocks. Not good rocks, useless fist sized rocks that clanged when struck with a shovel and send shock waves through your hands and wrists. I developed trigger finger. It's a real thing.

A week later, Holly stood at the edge of the pit watching as I poured concrete over contoured rebar and mesh. The materials had cost several hundred dollars but it had been Holly's suggestion to build the pond so it was unfair for her to carry on about it.

"It's pretty big," she said.
"If a job's worth doing, it's worth doing well."
"Sure. What are you going to do with all the dirt you've removed?"
"I don't know, maybe make a rockery."
"That sounds nice. Where are you going to get the rocks?"

"You can find rocks anywhere."

I located a few decent rocks down the creek behind our house. They were heavy and took about an hour each to roll up the hill. I positioned them around the pond. Very natural. It needed more rocks though. I searched the creek again, with a shovel this time, and dug up a few more. I positioned those aesthetically above and behind the other rocks with dirt in between. It needed more rocks.

"I think you have enough rocks," Holly commented as she fed our new Koi. She'd named one Gene Simmons and the other Glimmer - it had been a long day and I couldn't be bothered arguing. There were approximately two-hundred rocks of various size and shape. Some were a greyish colour, others bluish slate. My favourites were those with lichen and moss. I'd planted ferns and ivy between the larger rocks - the largest of which I moved into place using a pulley system devised between two trees after researching ancient Egyptian building practices. It had taken me several days but it was beautiful.

"What?"
"I said I think you have enough rocks." Holly replied.
"You can't possibly be serious. There's a space between the north rockery and west rockery that needs at least another five large rocks and ten average sized ones. I was also thinking of extending the South rockery all the way to the spitting duck."

It had become an obsession. Everywhere I went I thought, "that's a nice rock." I kept gloves in the car so I could stop and take rocks if nobody was looking. I spent a lot of time on the Geographic Information Systems website for our area. GIS is similar to Google Maps but shows an overlay of property lines. I planned routes well out of my way so I could drive near public creek beds and rivers. I had dreams about rocks and woke up thinking about rocks.

Rockeries appeared everywhere. The problem was that the rockeries looked so good, it made areas without a rockery look like they were missing something. I was working on a rockery near our driveway when I met Carl. It was Autumn.

I'd caught a few glimpses of him riding back and forth across his lawn on his ride-on mower as the trees between our properties shed their leaves. He was an old man. Late seventies I'd guess. He always wore the same blue shorts and never wore a shirt. His nipples hung from large saggy flaps, swinging and flopping as he rode over bumps and around turns.

I was rolling a rock into place when he just kind of appeared out of nowhere. Short men are very sneaky. That's why most of them are pick-pockets. Carl stretched his mouth into what I suppose he thought was a smile. It looked more like a grimace. His small teeth looked like the tombstones you see in old cowboy movies, tilted and discoloured, apart from one gleaming white one. It at least provided some distraction from his chest flaps. As did his Invicta watch. I don't like Invicta watches. I'm not a watch snob, I just don't like Invicta watches or the people who wear them. I realise there is a market for Invicta watches but there is also a market for singing fish. I sometimes flick over to the shopping channel where they sell Invicta Watches just so I can yell at the television.

"Up next, we have the Invicta Armada IV in 100% real gold plate. This stunning piece is almost as thick as it is wide, see how the dial covers our model's entire arm?"
"Oh my god! $699 or $30 per month over 24 months for that?"
Holly usually tells me to stop watching if it upsets me so much and I tell her that I just want to see the next one...
"Oh my god! ! It's worse than the previous one! Who is buying these dreadful things? The dial looks like a Ball jar lid and there are bits sticking out all over the place. Who needs twelve buttons on the side of a watch? I can't handle this."
"Then change the fucking channel. We're missing *Below Deck.*"
"I just want to see the next one.. Oh my god! Look at it!"

Below Deck is my favourite program on television which shows how much I dislike Invicta watches. Short men like Invicta watches. And child porn.

"Hi. I'm Carl."

"David. How do you do?" We shook hands.

"Good, good. I just wanted to ask if you knew where the property border is."

"Sorry?"

"The property border."

"Er, yes. It's near the tree line. Why?

"No, it actually runs parallel two feet from your driveway. All of these rocks are on my property."

"Are you serious?"

Carl frowned, "Yes, of course I'm serious."

"Actually, the property border *is* near the tree line," I corrected him, "There's a metal pole in the ground over there."

"No, that pole's wrong."

"Yes, I know. According to the Geographic Information System's website, the pole should be about eight feet closer to your house. I wasn't going to bother about it though, you know, because it would seem a bit petty."

Carl's face turned red and contorted with anger like one of those Indonesian god masks people hang on their walls near a big vase with wiggly sticks. A small version of the mask obviously, hung way too low. I was taken aback for a moment.

"Right! You want a fucking problem? You've got a fucking problem. We'll let the man deal with this."

"What man?" I asked, looking around.

"The man. The law. Are you stupid?"

"I've just never heard it called that before. Is it a Sixties thing?"

"Everyone calls it that."

"No, I'm pretty sure they don't."

"Yes they do."

"We've lived here twenty years," shouted Carl's wife.

She'd appeared from behind a tree like a magic elf. She was short and fat and had tight curly hair.

"Sorry?"

"We've lived here twenty years."

"What's that got to do with anything?"

Carl and his short fat wife stared at each other with their mouths open like those furry things on *Sesame Street* that try to communicate with a rotary telephone.

"We've lived here twenty years." she yelled again.

"Right, well I should probably get back to my rockery but it's been a pleasure. Brownies might be the traditional welcoming gift but having tiny lunatics yell at you about invisible lines and occupancy periods is probably the next best thing."

Short men don't like you turning your back to them. They need to be seen and heard. I glanced over my shoulder as I walked away to check Carl wasn't about to go all spider monkey on me but he was off - stomping away with his fists clenched and his elbows pointed out as if he was carrying two invisible buckets of water. Short men do this a lot. It's their version of an annoyed pufferfish. His short fat wife bounced after him. Carl started mowing a lot after that. Four or five times a week. He made a path through the trees between our houses so he could mow two feet from our driveway, scowling the whole time at my apparently infringing driveway rockery. I waved with a big smile whenever I saw him. He'd purse his lips, glare a bit and shake his head. It was the trees that pushed him over the edge though.

I planted twenty Leyland Cypress trees just our side of the metal pole. They're evergreens, in staggered formation, which means regardless of the season, we can step outside our front door or look out the kitchen window without seeing Carl's flappy torso zooming past. They're only four or five feet in height at the moment but I was told they grow fast. My friend JM is an expert on trees.

"Get yourself some Leyland Cypress trees. They grow fast. That will fix the problem."
"Really? How fast do they grow?"
"Oh, ten feet a year or so."
"That seems highly unlikely. Did you just make up a random number?"
"No, it was an estimate."

Carl stood on his back deck watching the nursery truck deliver the trees with his neck craned out like a turtle and his arms bent against the railing as if he was doing push ups. I waved and he went inside.

The problem with short men is that they always have something to prove. Nobody cares but as far as they're concerned, everybody has to. I saw a movie once called *The Incredible Shrinking Man* in which some guy ate something or got zapped and shrunk down to the size of a pea. There was a scene where he was trying to get the attention of his wife. He jumped up and down waving his arms around screaming, "Please notice me. I'm down here. For the love of god, please notice me." This is essentially how short men spend every waking hour. It's more of an internal jumping and yelling but it's there in every nuance.

The next morning, as I made coffee in the kitchen, I glanced out the window and noticed Carl had tied neon orange plastic ribbons on the Leyland Cypress trees closest to our driveway. The metal pole in the ground had been removed. I put on shoes and took my coffee and a pair of scissors outside. Carl watched me from his back deck so I gave him a friendly wave as I cut the last of the ribbons in my pyjamas. He didn't wave back. He stormed down his steps and across his yard.

"Morning Carl. Beautiful day, isn't it. I was just doing a bit of trimming."
"You actually just committed a crime. It's against the law to remove property markers."
He stood on one of my rocks and reached out to tap me on the shoulder, "I'm making a citizen's arrest."
"I don't think that's how it works," I said.

"Yes it is. I looked it up."

"Do I get a phone call? If so, I'm going to call the circus and tell them to come and collect their midget clown."

"I beg your pardon?" Carl spluttered, "I beg your pardthhh..." Carl's white tooth, on a pink partial plate, flew out of his mouth and landed in the driveway. He went to pick it up.

I shouldn't have stepped on it. I wasn't helping the situation and knew that even as I did it. It was a spur of the moment reaction without any possible benefit or advantage. When you find yourself in a idiotic situation though, the temptation to test how far the idiocy will stretch can be overwhelming.

"That's actually on my side of the property line, Carl. It's my scary little white plastic tooth now. I might even tie a little bit of orange ribbon around it."

Carl took his phone out of his pocket and flipped it open. Old people like flip phones for some reason. Holly's parents both own flip phones and even the mention of upgrading to a smart phone sends them into a panic.

"I need a keyboard. Smart phones don't have keyboards."

"Yes, they do. You press this icon and the ke..."

"I don't understand. Why are you doing this to me?

Carl jabbed buttons and waited, "Polithe pleathe."

Despite being under citizen's arrest, I left Carl to it and went inside. Holly was making coffee and had watched most of the exchange from the kitchen window.

"Look," I said, holding up my tooth, "We've got a spare in case either of us ever loses one."

"Just once," Holly sighed, "I would like to live somewhere where we get along with our neighbours."

"It's never going to happen. People are dreadful wherever you go. Or maybe it's just us. Same result though."

"You mean just you. I get along with people fine."

"You hate people more than I do."

"Yes, but I manage to get along with them. Without spending $800 on trees. Besides, if I didn't hate people, we wouldn't have anything in common."

"Are you saying the only reason we're together is because we hate everyone else?"

"Yes."

"What about pineapple on pizza? We both like pineapple on pizza."

"No, not really. I just put up with it because you like it."

"Right, well I'm not a massive fan of those pants you're wearing. I wasn't going to say anything but seeing how we're all opening up and being honest about things."

"I'm just saying, when you live in a small community, word gets around fast."

I printed off two copies of the Geographic Information Systems information for our area. I gave one to the officer when he arrived a short time later and the other to Carl's fat wife when he sent her down to ask for his tooth back. I'd thrown it in the bin but she waited while I dug it out. I put it in a sandwich bag for her as it was covered in oily cheese and cigarette ash. I added a bit of orange peel and a tea bag.

There were no more discussions about property lines after that but I don't wave to Carl anymore. I saw him kick our dog while it was playing in his yard. He kicked it hard enough to hurt and I heard the yelp all the way from our kitchen window. Short men like hurting animals. It's probably a DNA thing passed down from a time they weren't invited on mammoth hunts or something.

"Can I come?"
"No, you'll just get trampled. Stay here with the women and weave a basket or something. And stay away from the dog. Grok told me she saw you throwing rocks at it yesterday."
"I won't get trampled."
"To be honest, it's not your safety that's the issue. The other cavemen just find you kind of, well, annoying."
"In what way?"
"Just the whole thing really. Like the way you stick your elbows out when you walk."
"Do I? I hadn't noticed."
"Yes, it looks like you're carrying invisible buckets."
"What about Krog? He likes me."
"No, he doesn't."

I get along fine with our other neighbours though. I met

one of them a few weeks ago while I was adding to our letterbox rockery. When you live in a small community, word gets around fast.

"I heard you and Carl had some kind of falling out recently?"

"Yes, I caught him looking through our bathroom window while my wife was in the shower. He was standing on a stepladder. The police were involved."

"Oh my gosh. I saw the police car but had no idea."

"Yes, according to the officer, it's not the first time he's been in trouble for this kind of thing either."

"Really?"

"Yes, he's a registered sex offender. Carl's not even his real name. It's Steve."

"I always knew there was something about him. He's a very short man. So, I couldn't help but notice the accent. Australian?"

"Yes."

"Is your wife Australian as well?"

"No, she's very American."

"Really? Where did you meet?"

"Have you ever seen the television show *Below Deck*?"

"No."

"Well, I was working as a deck hand on a charter yacht and Holly was one of the guests..."

Disappointed

When I get older, I'm going to watch The Weather Channel a lot. If someone mentions that it's cold, or warm, or wet, I'll be able to tell them that a low front is moving in from the west which will give me an opening to be able to complain about my knees. And the price of ointments and balms these days. And the government.

....

From: Beverly Corrigan
Date: Thursday 21 November 2013 7.08pm
To: David Thorne
Subject: Very disappointed

Dear Mr Thorne,

On the 18th of November, I ordered two of your books from Amazon. *The Internet is a Playground* and *I'll Go Home Then, It's Warm And Has Chairs*. They were for my 14yo grandson. Both books are being returned immediately.

Good writers do not need to use foul language several times in the first few pages. It isn't clever, it just displays a limited vocabulary. At the very least, the cover should include a warning that the book contains explicit language so people don't have to waste their valuable time returning items. Thank you for your time.

Beverly Corrigan

....

From: David Thorne
Date: Friday 22 November 2013 2.14pm
To: Beverly Corrigan
Subject: Re: Very disappointed

Dear Beverly,

I'm sorry to hear of your disappointment. Hopefully Amazon's efficient return process won't interrupt your admonishment schedule too much. I'm sure you will let them know if it does.

As misery loves company, you may be pleased to learn that I have received similar correspondence from readers in the past. In response to this feedback, it may also please you to learn that reworked stories from the first two books are being released as a single volume targeted specifically towards your demographic. Available in both Block and Edison Disk Audio-book versions, the Victorian Edition is sure to be a hit at local council meetings, doctor's waiting rooms and church fundraisers.

Please find attached a few sample pages for your consideration.

Regards, David.

Overdue Account

"Hello David," said Jane, "can I have some money?"
"I haven't any," replied David, "but you can
have this picture of a spider I drew."
Jane looked at the drawing. It wasn't very good.
"No thanks," she said.

18

Artwork

"Do you like the picture I drew?" asked Martin.
"Yes," replied David, "it looks like it is in 3D."
"That's because I used drop-shadows," Martin explained.
Martin is an expert at the Adobe.

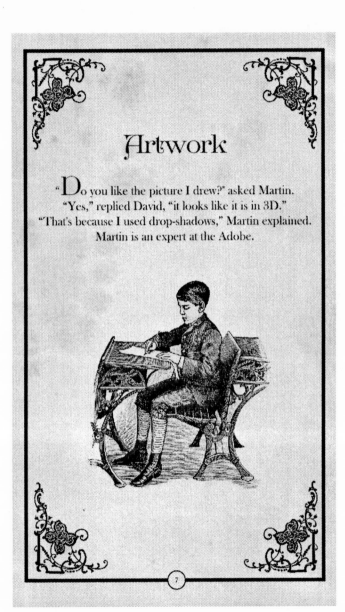

7

Tamra

She felt his lips against hers but little more.
It was like being kissed by her brother.
Somewhere along the way, the spark had gone out.
"Would you like it if I dressed up in outfits
for you? she suggested, "I could order
something online."
"Don't be silly," her father replied,
"that's money that could go towards fixing
the truck."

57

172

Astronomy

She pointed to another bright cluster,
"And what's that one called?"
"That's Magnus Centauri Beta Twelve," replied Mark,
"it's part of the Nebula Proxima Spiral."
He shivered and rubbed his hands together,
"We should go inside soon, I forgot to bring a jumper."
He had run out of space-sounding words and
feared she would catch on any minute.
"What about that one?" she asked.
Mark rubbed his hands together harder,
"That's Magnus Centauri Beta Thirteen."

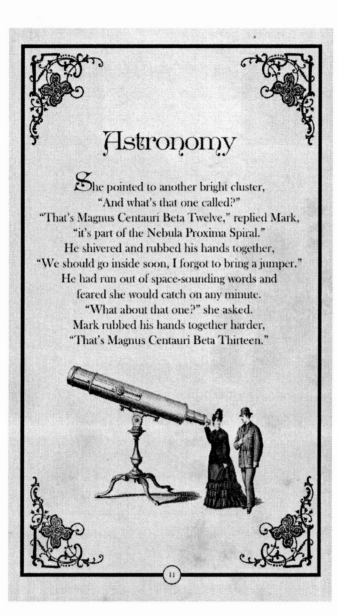

11

Lies

"It's a beautiful day," said Nick,
"we should have bought the kite."
"Yes," replied Kim. If Nick moved a little closer
to the edge, she thought, she could kick out
with both legs and he would roll off the cliff.
It would look like an accident.
Then, before anyone arrived, she would climb
down and slap his dead face.

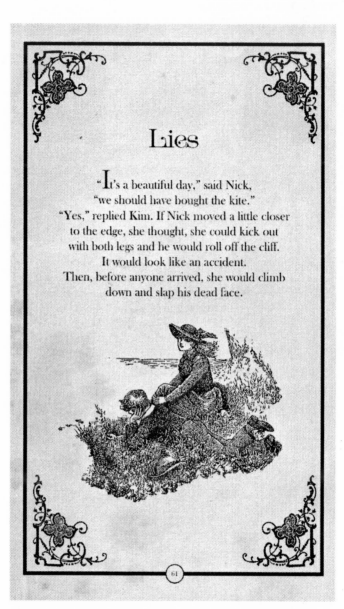

61

174

Bob's Files

Robert slammed the receipt and
chip packet onto the counter.
"I would like to exchange this packet of chips
for a new packet," he declared.
"This receipt is two years old," replied the assistant,
"and the packet is empty. Did you eat them?"
"Right," said Robert, "I'd like to speak to
the manager, please."

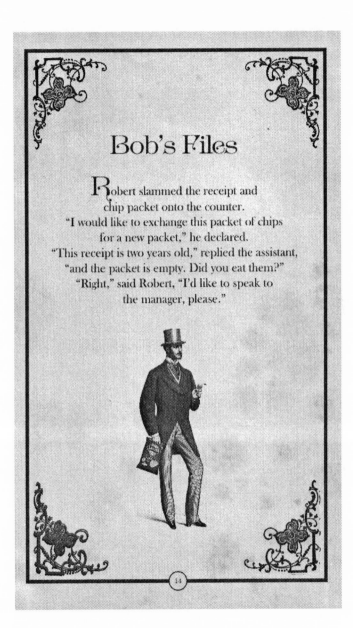

14

Bouncy Castle

The bouncy castle was a huge hit
at his birthday party.
Kevin jumped and jumped.
At his zenith, he could see clear over the fence.
"I'm a bird," he yelled, flapping his arms
while jumping from side to side.
Thankfully, nobody else had shown up
so there was plenty of room and
no one got hurt.

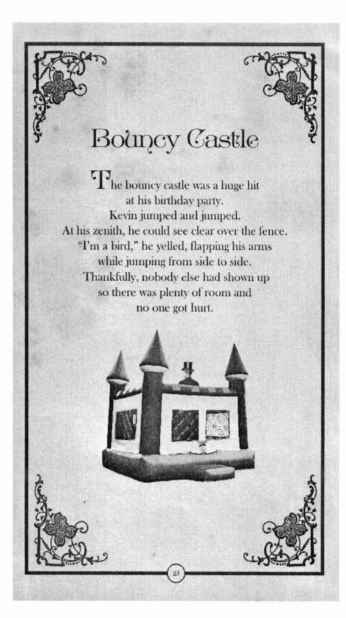

Skymall

The box was heavy.
Its contents were hidden by colourful
wrapping but she knew what it was.
She had hinted for months about the crystal carafe.
Henry watched her tear off the ribbon
and paper excitedly. He knew she would love the
cast iron paper towel holder shaped like a giraffe.
She'd been hinting for months.

20

Mammoths

"No thank you," said Professor Smith politely.
Professor Lewis looked puzzled.
He offered the plate again.
"I'm really not that hungry," said Professor Smith,
"I had a big lunch."
"You said you would eat it if I did," replied Professor
Lewis, "and it took me an hour to cook it.
Just try a little bit. For science."

15   15

Blockbuster

Megan pressed eject.
Why, she wondered, didn't Kevin Costner
just stay on the island with Jeanne Tripplehorn
and that girl from Napoleon Dynamite?
He would have gotten used to the land after
a while. Also, what where those flappy
bits of skin on his neck?
This shouldn't have been in the romantic
comedy section.

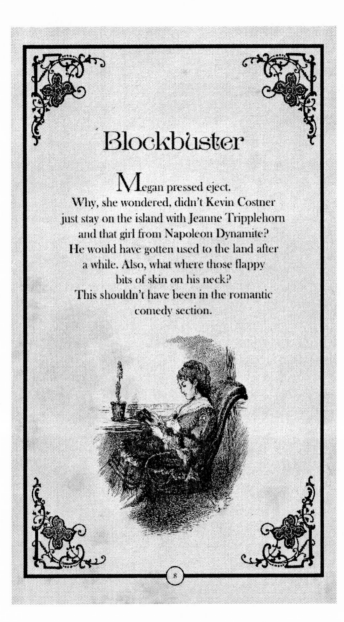

From: Beverly Corrigan
Date: Friday 22 November 2013 4.36pm
To: David Thorne
Subject: Re: Re: Very disappointed

I won't be buying that book either I'm afraid. It's sad that this is what passes for humour these days.

Beverly Corrigan

Beverly's Window

Beverly threw open the curtains. Light flooded the room. Outside, children laughed as they raced by on bicycles, couples walked hand in hand, and music could be heard softly in the distance.

Today was the day of the parade.

"We'll be having none of that," said Beverly as she closed the curtains and reinserted the carrot.

From: Beverly Corrigan
Date: Friday 22 November 2013 7.22pm
To: David Thorne
Subject: Re: Re: Re: Re: Very disappointed

I'm reporting you to my internet service provider.

JC Penney

My partner Holly works for a bank. Not one of the big banks, a small bank with only a few branches. Big banks have large glossy posters of happy people buying houses, driving new cars, and giving children wizzies. The posters in Holly's bank are black and white A4 printouts featuring gardening clipart. The customer service desks are dark wood and the carpets are dark green. According to Holly, it's like the bank in *It's a Wonderful Life* but I don't watch black and white movies because I own a colour television and it's not 1945 so I'll have to take her word on it.

Mirroring the bank's main customer demographic, the people who work there are religious and old. They attend church, grow cabbages, and watch the Weather Channel. The men wear vests under double-breasted suit jackets two sizes too large for them, the women wear pleated polyester dresses with flower patterns.

"You should find out the combination to the safe," I said to Holly, "It could be our retirement plan. We'll empty it out and live on the run."
"I don't need a combination," she replied, "They never lock it."

We were at one of several annual functions for her work.

They'd hired a staff member's John Denver cover band for the occassion and there was a makeshift bar, with a two drink maximum, tended by a weird little man and his round little wife. The weird little man had retired from the bank years before but he liked being the bartender. He had nothing else to do and nobody had the heart to tell him to fuck off. His round little wife looked like a Muppet. Not one of the main Muppets, a Muppet Jim Henson might have thrown together on an off day using left over round bits.

"That's an interesting one Mr Henson. What's its name?"
"Oh, I don't know... Muppet thing."

Everything seemed to be in slow motion. And muffled, and grey. Most of the people worked together so stood around in awkward small groups, occasionally becoming animated when someone thought of something to say but for the most part just pretending to listen to the band. The lead singer of the band, a man in his eighties, wore large orange tinted glasses and a tan suede vest. He mumbled the words to the songs rather than singing them. It was like a stroke victim reading aloud from a book, accompanied by a guitar, drums, and a stick with bottlecaps nailed to it. The beat seemed random but there was one lady dancing. She had her hands held up in front of her, like a mime doing the invisible glass thing, and was walking in circles.

"Look at that one dancing. It's like Helen Keller trapped in a closet. Someone should do something about it."

"Like what?" Holly asked.

"Like leave. *Below Deck* starts in twenty minutes. This is the saddest event I have ever been to. And that includes funerals and Thanksgiving dinners at your parent's house."

The only thing edible at Holly's parent's Thanksgiving dinners are the Dry Balls. Dry Balls are basically bits of bread dipped in milk, rolled into a ball, and baked. Which may sound dreadful, but they come with a cold white sauce made of milk and flour that helps you swallow them. I usually get McDonald's on the way. After everyone finishes eating, we sit in the living room watching The Weather Channel for an hour or two in silence. Occasionally someone will comment on how good the Dry Balls were but conversation is kept to a minimum as Holly's father Tom, who is going deaf, makes a big production of turning the television sound down every time someone speaks then turning it back up to its highest setting when they have finished.

"The Dry Balls were good this year, Tom"

"What?"

"The Dry Balls."

"Hang on," ▮▮▮▮▬▬▬ "What?"

"I was just saying the Dry Balls were particularly good this year. Best Dry Balls I've ever had in fact."

"What about the Dry Balls?"

"They were good."

"Marie, what did he say?"

"He said the Dry Balls were good."

"Oh." ▂▃▄▅▆▇

"We can't leave yet. They're giving out certificates in a minute."

"Gift certificates?"

"No. Just certificates. For people who have been at the bank for twenty years or more."

"Do they get anything else?"

"No, like what?"

"I don't know. Something good. It's just a certificate stating so and so has been working for the bank for twenty years?"

"It's framed." Holly replied.

Oh, well that's alright then. If I worked somewhere for twenty years and they gave me an *unframed* certificate stating that I had worked there for twenty years, I'd be a little disappointed. They're nice frames then?"

"They're plastic. But they look like wood. We can leave after they give them out."

"Fine. Just don't leave me standing here alone again."

"There was a line at the bathroom."

"Some old lady trapped me in a corner for several minutes while you were gone. She explained her views on having a 'coloured' family in the Whitehouse. I asked her if she had ever seen two dogs kiss."

"What?"

"You know, when they touch noses and both stick out their tongues at the same time."

"I work with these people. Who was it?"

"I don't know, they all look the same. She had really tight skin, it was pulled back so far her gums were showing. It looked like she was wearing one of those things dentists put in your mouth. An invisible one though. She had a walking frame."

"That's Sue."

"I didn't even get to drink my second beer. I put it down on a table for just a second and an old man with sores all over his face put his down as well. I picked up what I thought was mine and took a sip but it tasted like mint denture paste so I spat it back into the bottle."

"So you asked Sue if she'd ever seen two dogs kiss and then you spat into a bottle?"

"Yes."

"Right, well I won't be leaving your side again. It's like having a child with Autism."

"It's pronounced Altruism."

"No it isn't. Just try to act normal for the next half hour or so. And please don't steal anything. It isn't funny."

"I have to I'm afraid, it's the rules."

The rules had been written years before I met Holly. I was at my friend Geoffrey's house one day and he was being annoying so on my way out, I took a painting from his hallway wall. I'm not sure why, I just thought it would be funny for Geoffrey to walk down his hallway and see a blank space where it had been. It was a terrible painting - Geoffrey had painted it himself - showing a knight in armour standing on the top of a mountain raising his sword to a

187

stormy sky. Apparently it was a self portrait but the face looked more like a monkey. Geoffrey called it *Journey's End* but I referred to it as *Monkey Being Dangerous*.

"The title doesn't make any sense."

"Yes it does."

"No it doesn't, sooner or later the monkey is going to have to walk back down the mountain so it should really be called, *Journey's Half Way Point* or, *That Was a Bit Pointless, Good Exercise Though.*"

"It's not a monkey and the journey is over because it was a journey of discovery. The fact he has to go back down the mountain afterwards doesn't come into it. Besides, he can ride back down."

"On what?"

"His horse."

"Where's his horse?"

"It's behind that big rock. You can see its head sticking out a little bit."

"Oh yeah. I can kind of see the horse's body as well. Is the rock semi-transparent?"

"No, I painted the horse first but it didn't look right so I painted the rock over it but the horse was black so it shows through a little bit. I should go over it again sometime."

"Or you could just rename it, *Journey to the Semi-Transparent Rock.*"

Geoffrey came to my house a few hours later to recover the painting, it was hanging in my living room above the fireplace. On his way out, he pocketed the remote control for my television.

Rules had to be defined after this; you can't take anything that the person uses regularly and it has to be obvious. Their favourite mug that you would use the next time they visited, the welcome mat, all their cutlery apart from teaspoons. Eventually it became a reason to visit each other.

"I wasn't going to drop in but I really needed my bathroom soap dispenser back. Hey, what's that over there?"
"What?"
"Oh, I thought I saw something. Well, I should be off."

The game spread outside our homes. I'd visit Geoffrey at his work and the secretary would ask him later if he knew what happened to the clock on the wall behind her desk, he'd visit my work and a potted plant would go missing. It progressed to work related functions where we no longer took items from each other, but competed.

"What did you get?"
"A serving bowl shaped like a duck."
"Nice."
"You?"
"The little brass bell from the foyer. And a lamp."

Eventually, it became the only real reason to attend functions and we saw it as a kind of recompense for having to be there.

It wasn't Kleptomania, the items made their way back eventually, but it was close. We couldn't walk into a room without automatically scanning everything in it and calculating the probability of successfully concealing each item under our jacket.

"I might even steal one of the certificates." I said to Holly. She laughed.

"Oh no. Here comes your friend," I warned, "She's very slowly headed our way."

"Hello Sue," said Holly, "How are you?"

"Oh, I can't complain." said Sue, "I'm having a better week than Janet in accounting. Have you heard? Her husband had an affair."

"Was it with a coloured woman?" I asked.

Sue frowned, "No, I don't think so."

"Well that's something."

"This is my husband David," Holly interjected, "He's Australian. David, this is Sue."

"Yes, we've met," said Sue, "I didn't realise he was Australian though. I just thought he had a speech impediment."

She looked me up and down, "You don't look Australian. Australian men are usually blonde. And rugged."

"Do you own seventy cats?"

"No, just two."

"Well there you go. You can't judge a book by its cover. Have you ever seen them kiss?"

"No."

"They probably only do it when you're not looking."

Sue glanced at Holly. Holly pretended to be intensely interested in her glass of wine.

"There was one Australian man I liked," Sue continued, "What was his name..?"

"Was it Pat?"

"No. The one who got stabbed by a swordfish. He was married to an American girl as well. Did you know him?"

"Steve Irwin? Yes, we were good friends before the swordfish thing. Only it wasn't a swordfish. It was a starfish."

"No, they weren't," said Holly.

Sue looked puzzled.

"He didn't know Steve Irwin. He's joking."

Sue's eyes narrowed, "Oh really. What do you do David? Are you a clown?"

"Of sorts. What do you do Sue? Work in a wind tunnel?"

Sue turned to Holly, "You couldn't find a nice American boy to settle down with?"

When people ask where my wife and I met, I generally make up something - we met at space camp, or a rodeo, or were the only two that turned up to a group counselling session for borderline Agoraphobia. It gives them something to talk about later. I'd told half the people I spoke to that night it was, "kind of like in the movie *Pretty Woman*, except I'm Julia Roberts," and the other half that we met on the set of *So You Think You Can Dance*.

'Oh, you're a dancer?"

"Yes. It's my craft."

"What kind of dance?"
"Name one."
"Modern?"
"Yes, that's it."

The truth is, Holly and I met spelunking. My torch dimmed and she had a spare set of batteries. Afterwards, we had drinks and got along well. She was American, visiting Australia on a work visa, I was working for a small branding agency called de Masi jones at the time. We were rarely apart after that. We moved in together, married, moved countries, and bought a house. Other stuff happened between that stuff obviously but it was just the normal stuff; walks along the beach, eating spaghetti like the two dogs in that cartoon about two dogs, spinning clay pots etc.

We also had to go through the whole immigration process which consists of completing several hundred forms with accompanying supporting documents, writing cheques, and attending interviews in which we were tested, in separate rooms, to see if we were really living as a married couple.

"What side of the bed does your wife sleep on?"
"From which direction?"
"Sorry?"
"Looking out from in bed, Holly is on my left. But if you were standing at the foot of the bed looking at us, I'd be on your left."
"No, you do it like a car. From where you're sitting.

"Oh, that makes sense."

"So your answer is left?"

"Actually, it's more in the middle. I usually only have a few feet or so. On the right. Although, sometimes she sleeps diagonally."

I'll just mark it down as left. Next question. Describe your bed linen."

"Wrinkly."

I think you are meant to take it out of the dryer as soon as it stops spinning but who does that? It's like leaving the dishwasher and washing machine open when you are not using them so they don't get smelly. Who's walking around their house as if everything is perfectly normal with appliance doors open?

Holly pulled me through a sea of oversized grey suits and polyester ankle length pleated dresses towards the bar.

"She seemed nice," I said.

Holly gave me a dirty look, "She works down the hall from me. All I asked was for you to be normal for thirty minutes."

"Why did you tell her that I wasn't friends with Steve Irwin? I was going to make up a whole thing about packs of starfish terrorising Australian beach communities."

"Yes, I've already been asked twice if we really met on the set of *So You Think You Can Dance*."

"Nobody asked about the movie *Pretty Woman*?"

"What?"

"Nothing."

"No, what about *Pretty Woman*?"

"Someone asked me where we met and I told them it was kind of like the movie *Pretty Woman*."

"You told people I work with that I was a prostitute?"

"No, I said *I* was Julie Roberts."

"Oh my god."

"It gives them something to talk about. Something apart from Wheel of Fortune and what they read in this year's Farmer's Almanac. Old people crave gossip. It's like crack to them. Take away gossip at their age and they'd have nothing."

The weird little man behind the bar filled Holly's glass of wine and handed it to her with a creepy smile. The top half of his body was normal shaped, fairly slim for a man in his seventies, but from his waist down, he had a fat woman's body. He was wearing 'mum pants' that were tight in the crotch and actually had a kind of flat, wide, camel toe. He was also wearing an 'official bartender' badge that he had made himself.

"Just a beer thanks." I told him.

"No, sorry, you've already had two."

"It must have been someone who looks like me, I just got here."

"No, it was you."

"Any beer is fine."

"This is my husband David," Holly said, "He's Australian. David, this is Tim."

We shook hands. He had the short man handshake; squeezy like it's a competition.

"Nice to meet you, Tim. I'm fairly sure one of those Amstel Lights in the cooler behind you has my name on it."

"There's a two drink maximum."

"It's for a friend. Who hasn't had any yet."

"No, it isn't."

"Fine. I have had two but I didn't get to drink my second one. Some old man with sores on his face mixed our drinks up and I got the one with denture spit in it."

"That's not my fault. You should have kept an eye on it."

"Just give me a beer."

"There's a two drink maximum."

"Right, well I commend you on taking your job so seriously, I see you made yourself a little badge and everything, but the moment you're not watching, I'm taking an Amstel light."

Tim turned to the large cooler on the counter behind him, closed the lid and snapped the clasp shut. While he did so, I grabbed a bottle of Stella Artois from the counter in front. He turned back.

"That foiled my plans." I told him, "You're like Kevin Costner in that movie. The one where he protects Whitney Houston and they fall in love, not the one where he swims a lot."

I raised my Stella in salute.

"Where did you get that?" Tim asked, "Did you take it off the counter?"

"This? No, an older boy gave it to me."

"I see you've met Holly's husband David," said Sue.

She'd followed us through the crowd like the robot cowboy in the movie *West World* and, if you were to put Yul Bryner in a wispy grey wig and under twenty G's acceleration, they'd look like identical twins.

"Yes," said Tim, "David was just about to ask me for a bottle opener."
"No, it's a twist off."
"David tells jokes did you know?" Sue continued. She looked at me, "Tell Tim the one about Steve Irwin."
"It wasn't really a joke," I replied, " I just said that I knew him and it's tragic he died."
"Oh," said Tim, "You knew Steve Irwin?"
"No," explained Sue, "Apparently that's the joke. He didn't actually know Steve Irwin."

Sue and Tim stared at each other for a moment. It was if they were communicating telepathically and I think there was a little nod.

"Tell us another joke, David," Sue said.

When I was about eight or nine, there was a boy in my class named Patrick who told a joke one day to a group of us in the playground. It was a dirty joke and we all giggled because it had the word vagina in it. I didn't get the joke but I laughed anyway so as not to appear stupid. Everyone encouraged Patrick to tell it again and he did. I still didn't get it and had my suspicions that the only reason everyone told him to repeat it is because they didn't get it either. Patrick was the star of the day and he told the same joke about twenty times during break. The next day during lunch, about ten people asked me if I wanted to hear the same joke. By the third day, everybody had heard it so everybody was telling it to somebody who had already heard it. It was about a week later, during 'religion studies' class, that I suddenly realised Patrick had been telling the joke wrong. Nobody hearing or telling joke 'got it' because somehow Patrick had fucked up the punch line. The punchline wasn't, "Can I smell your feet then?", it had to be, "Oh, it must be your feet then."

I leant over to where Patrick was sitting at the desk in front of me and tapped him on the back.

"It's not '*Can* I smell your feet then?' I told him, "It's, 'Oh, it *must* be your feet then', you told it wrong."

"No," he said, "my way is better."

"What?"

"My way is much funnier."

"Your way doesn't make any sense. You've been telling it wrong the whole time."

"What doesn't make any sense?" the boy sitting next to Patrick asked. His name was Adam but everyone called him Nits because he once had hair lice.

"Patrick told the joke wrong," I said, "It's not, 'Can I smell your feet then?', it's, 'Oh, it must be your feet then.'"

"No, " said Nits, "Patricks way is heaps funnier."

An argument broke out.

"Right," yelled the teacher. He was an elderly chaplain that only taught the one class. "David, Patrick, Adam. What seems to be the problem? Why aren't you quietly colouring in your picture of Jesus healing a beggar? Stand up please."

We stood.

"Come on out with it."

"David says Patrick told a joke wrong," Nits declared, "But he didn't."

"What joke?"

The three of us stared at each other, eyes wide in panic.

"David, what's the joke?"

"Um..."

"Right now please."

"A man and a lady get into an elevator and the man says, "Can I smell your... um... thingy?" and the lady says, "No, certainly not." and the man says..."

"RIGHT!"

All three of us had to stay in during recess and write, "Jesus hears everything we say," fifty times each on the blackboard. If this was true, Jesus must have been pretty exasperated at hearing the joke told wrong thousands of times. At the end of recess, as we headed off to our next class, the chaplain called me back and asked me what the punchline was. It must have been bothering him. I told him and he didn't laugh but his lips quivered a bit.

"Okay," I said to Sue and Tim, "A man and a lady get into an elevator and the man says..."

Holly's eyes widened in horror and she shook her head. She'd heard the joke. I was thrown for a second. I had nothing.

"er..."

"Yes?" asked Sue.

"...the man says, "I really like your dress. Is that Rayon?" and the lady says, "No, I think it's Polyester, I got it from JC Penney.""

Tim laughed for a second and then frowned. Sue just frowned.

"That's more of a conversation than a joke," she said.

"Yes, I suppose so."

"You're really quite bad at telling jokes. Buying a dress from JC Penney isn't funny."

"No, I suppose not. It's quite sad in fact. JC Penney is dreadful."

"My dress is from JC Penny," Sue said.

"Well there you go."

The John Denver cover band was cut off as the president of the bank took over the stage. The bottlecap-stick player seemed a bit annoyed by this as he was in the middle of a solo. The president tapped the microphone a couple of times and asked for everyone's attention.

"Firstly, a big hand for Brian and his band, The Rocking Mountain Highs. They certainly are 'rocking' the roof tonight."

The audience clapped politely. A few people acknowledged

the pun with a chuckle. Tim laughed loudly for about three seconds too long.

"Secondly, um, Tim would like me to remind everyone that there is a two drink maximum at the bar. This the eighth year in a row Tim has helped out behind the bar since retiring and we really appreciate his efforts."

The audience clapped again, though not quite as enthusiastically this time. It wasn't just me who thought the function would be a lot better if Tim fucked off and died. Tim acknowledged the crowd with a big wave and a little bow as if he had just been elected Mayor of the village.

If I was the village Mayor, I would make it a law that everyone had to punch Tim at least once a week. And that everyone had to give me money and bring me stuff. I'd actually be the worst person I can think of to be put in a position of power. It's said that power corrupts and absolute power corrupts absolutely but I'd be at that absolutely corrupted bit well before I got anywhere near the absolute power part.

"Right, I'd like to welcome you all tonight. It's been an exciting year at the bank. We have a few new faces and said goodbye to a few old ones. Tonight is to thank those who have been with us for many years so without, any, um, further ado..." He tucked the microphone under his arm while unfolding a piece of paper and putting on a pair of reading glasses, "We have four people celebrating decade milestones this year. First up, Margaret Yoder has been with the bank twenty years. Come on up, Margaret."

The audience clapped as Margaret leapt excitedly onto the stage and accepted her framed certificate. She held it over her head like she'd just won a silver dish at the Wimbledon women's finals as a friend of hers took a photo. You're probably thinking I'm exaggerating and if not, I should feel bad for belittling something that means so much to someone. You'd be wrong on both accounts. Margaret leapt off stage with her hands held high and her legs tucked up behind her. She froze mid jump and the chorus from 'Can't Stop Us Now' played. Okay, that last bit *was* exaggerated but it was kind of like that.

"Thank you, Margaret. Next up, we have the first of two thirty-year veterens, Nora Peterson. Nora has been a teller since starting at the bank in 1984. Wow, 1984, it only seems like a blink of an eye ago, doesn't it? "

Nora climbed the stage to collect her framed thirty year certificate as people clapped and nodded agreement to each other that 1984 did indeed seem like only a blink of an eye ago. Most of them had the same haircut they had in 1984. And 1974. Nora didn't seem quite as impressed as Margaret had been with her certificate. Her first name was misspelt as Norp. She smiled gracefully but it seemed a bit forced. A few people had to rush to steady her as she stumbled on the steps leaving the stage.

"Our second 'thirty yearer' is Grace Chapman. Grace isn't here tonight as she is in hospital having surgery on her knee but we're sure she will be back behind the counter in no time. Let's all take a moment to send a prayer her way."

The bank president clasped his hands at his crotch and lowered his head with his eyes closed. Everyone in the crowd did the same thing.

"Dear Father, we ask you to cast a special eye over one of your flock tonight."
"What the fuck?" I asked Holly.
"Shhh."
"We pray that Grace's knee surgery will go well without any complications or infections and that she has a speedy recovery. Thank you, Lord. Amen."

The prayer lasted almost long enough for me to slip behind the bar and get an Amstel Light - and the bottle opener because it wasn't a twist-off. Tim opened his eyes to discover me mid pop. I thought it was the rules that everyone had to keep their eyes closed until after the Amen bit. I have no idea how these things work as these things aren't done in Australia. In Australia, if someone suggested everyone at a function prayed, there would be a fair amount of laughter and someone would yell, "Good one, dickhead."

"I'll accept the certificate on Grace's behalf and get right to our final certificate recipient, Sue McKenzie. This is Sue's fiftieth year at the bank starting as a teller in 1964. In 1987, she was promoted to the loan application department where she has been ever since. Come on up, Sue."

The audience clapped. Sue beamed - which stepped her teeth-baring up a notch - and, with some assistance, climbed the steps. She waited patiently while the president's personal secretary whispered something in his ear. He nodded and turned back to the microphone.

"Um, we seem to have misplaced Sue's certificate. If everyone could have a quick look around their tables and seats... No? Well, I'm sure it will turn up. Thank you, Sue."